100
favorite
VERSES FROM THE
BOOK OF MORMON

TABLE OF

CONTENTS

OBEDIENCE

And it came to pass that I, Nephi, said unto my father: I will go and do the things which the Lord hath commanded, for I know that the Lord giveth no commandments unto the children of men, save he shall prepare a way for them that they may accomplish the thing which he commandeth them.

1 Ne. 3:7

In this simple declaration of faith and obedience, we hear no hesitation, no doubt, no expression of fear, no murmuring about the difficulty of the commandment. Rather, we hear an affirmation of faith and a positive plan of action, the key to which involves the words *go* and *do*. Whatever the Lord asks of us, He expects us to be up and doing. While our own personal tests of obedience may not involve traversing a rough and difficult terrain fraught with physical dangers, they do require us to keep putting one faithful foot in front of the other, trusting in the promises of the Lord.

When we reach out to the Lord and endeavor to keep His commandments, we are rewarded beyond our greatest expectations—not necessarily with worldly goods, but with peace, comfort, and the reassuring knowledge of God's love and concern. For every step we are willing to take toward our Savior, He gladly meets us more than halfway. This reassurance is found time and again in the scriptures. In our day we are told, "Be faithful and diligent in keeping the commandments of God, and I will encircle thee in the arms of my love" (D&C 6:20).

As our spirits respond in obedience to God's commandments, we rejoice in the promises found in Isaiah 58:8–11: "Then shall thy light break forth as the morning, and thine health shall spring forth speedily: and thy righteousness shall go before thee; the glory of the Lord shall be thy rereward. Then shalt thou call, and the Lord shall answer; thou shalt cry, and he shall say, Here I am. . . . And the Lord shall guide thee continually . . . and thou shalt be like a watered garden, and like a spring of water, whose waters fail not."

> *For every step we are willing to take toward our Savior, He gladly meets us more than halfway.*

Nephi reaffirms this promise: "And thus we see that the commandments of God must be fulfilled. And if it so be that the children of men keep the commandments of God he doth nourish them, and strengthen them, and provide means whereby they can accomplish the thing which he has commanded them" (1 Ne. 17:3).

Rather than being restrictive, the principle of obedience affords us greater freedoms. We bask in the Lord's promise of eternal safety and peace, and our spirits are continually refreshed by His rich showers of blessings.

PRAYER

And I said unto them: Have ye inquired of the Lord?

1 NE. 15:8

This simple yet profound question has meaning for every child of God. It is through prayer that we receive comfort in times of sorrow and loss, answers to life's puzzling and often painful dilemmas, courage to face challenges that would be otherwise overwhelming and insurmountable, and the priceless gift of a testimony of our Savior's love and of the precious truths of His gospel.

At times we may wonder whether He is there and listening. This poignant question is echoed in a beloved Primary song, and it carries with it a resounding answer. Yes, He is there. The Savior reassures us of this eternal truth. "Pray always, and I will pour out my spirit upon you, and great shall be your blessing—yea, even more than if you should obtain treasures of earth" (D&C 19:38).

Is there any prayer too trivial, too insignificant? The prophet Alma admonishes us to "call upon his holy name" at all times and for all things—morning, midday, and evening prayers for the successful daily operation of our households; for protection from our enemies and the adversary; for prosperity in our professions and occupations; for well-being for ourselves, our families, and our friends; and for mercy for our wrongdoings and shortcomings (see Alma 34:17–27).

The power of prayer should never be underestimated, and the power of the prayer of a righteous woman is awe-inspiring. Her petitions in behalf of her loved ones bring answers and blessings worthy of note. Hannah, Sariah, Ruth, Elizabeth, Mary, Abish, the mothers of the stripling warriors, Lucy Mack, Emma Smith—these and countless other righteous daughters of God set an example of the power of prayer for women everywhere.

> *The power of prayer should never be underestimated.*

And the sweet assurance found in Doctrine and Covenants 112:10 is a promise that all—men, women, and children alike—can claim: "Be thou humble; and the Lord thy God shall lead thee by the hand, and give thee answer to thy prayers."

Elder Jeffrey R. Holland reminds us that in answer to our earnest and heartfelt prayers, the Holy Ghost will reveal to both our minds and our hearts the reassuring and reasonable answers from our Heavenly Father (see Trusting Jesus *[Salt Lake City: Deseret Book, 2003], 172).*

FRIENDSHIP

3

Think of your brethren like unto yourselves, and be familiar with all and free with your substance, that they may be rich like unto you.

JACOB 2:17

The use of the word *brethren* in this scripture carries with it the connotation of friendship and the sharing of our substance—a broad interpretation that goes far beyond our material goods.

The Savior said, "come, follow me" (Luke 18:22). As in all things, His example of friendship is perfect. During His earthly ministry He was a friend to poor and rich alike, to those who were easy to love and those who were not so easy to love, to those whose lives were touched by sin as well as those whose lives were exemplary, to those who were sick and afflicted by every imaginable infirmity as well as to those who were whole and well and strong. He offered friendship to those with questionable occupations as well as to those with solid social standings, to those of differing racial and cultural groups as well as to those whose heritage was like His own.

Elder Neal A. Maxwell said, "You and I are believers in and preachers of a glorious gospel that can deepen all human relationships now as well as projecting friendships into eternity. Friendships, as well as families, are forever" (*All These Things Shall Give Thee Experience* [Salt Lake City: Deseret Book, 1979], 56).

A radiant smile, a sincere expression of concern, a listening ear that is not mindful of the ticking of the clock, a heart that hears what is hidden beneath the words, lips that are fastened against hasty expressions of judgment—these are all Christlike gestures of friendship that link our hearts and spirits in friendship with our children, our siblings, our parents, our spouses, our coworkers, our neighbors, the stranger in need, and thus with the Savior Himself.

> *Can there be a greater gift than to be the Lord's friend?*

The Savior said, "I will call you friends, for you are my friends, and ye shall have an inheritance with me" (D&C 93:45). To be the Lord's friend and have an inheritance with Him—can there be a greater gift bestowed upon us?

We read in Proverbs 17:17 that "A friend loveth at all times," not just when it is easy or convenient. This is the measure of the Lord's friendship and sets the standard for our own.

✿

As mankind's greatest Friend, the Savior freely shares that which is most precious—His love, His tender mercy, His redeeming gospel. Can we as His friends do any less?

SERVICE

*And behold, I tell you these things that ye may learn wisdom;
that ye may learn that when ye are in the service of your fellow beings ye are only in the service of your God.*

MOSIAH 2:17

These inspired and inspiring words of a great prophet-king are echoed in the words of the hymn, "A Poor Wayfaring Man of Grief":

> Then in a moment to my view
> The stranger started from disguise.
> The tokens in His hands I knew;
> The Savior stood before mine eyes.
> He spake, and my poor name he named,
> "Of me thou hast not been ashamed.
> These deeds shall my memorial be;
> Fear not, thou didst them unto me" (*Hymns*, no. 29).

Opportunities for service abound, whether they be in our families, our church, our neighborhood, or our community. True service is selfless and is rendered with a glad heart and a willing spirit rather than out of a sense of duty. It is not something to cross off our "how to get to heaven" checklist. It is done without fanfare, occasionally anonymously, often without recognition—sometimes even without thanks.

As parents, we serve our families daily and in countless ways. Does it make a difference? Does anyone notice? The impact may not be immediate, but in days and years to come, our children will feel touched and blessed by what we have done, and they in turn will have the pattern in place for their own selfless acts of service.

As we serve one another, we come to understand that the ultimate recipient is the Savior. He tells us, "Inasmuch as ye have done it unto one of the least of these . . . ye have done it unto me" (Matt. 25:40).

> As we serve one another, we come to understand that the ultimate recipient is the Savior.

❧

Think on the powerful advice from President Gordon B. Hinckley, who admonishes us to reach out to our brothers and sisters, to be keenly aware of their needs—whether physical, emotional, or spiritual—and to nurture them accordingly (see "Reach with a Rescuing Hand," Ensign, Nov. 1996, 86).

H E A R H I M

And now, he imparteth his word by angels unto men, yea, not only men but women also. Now this is not all; little children do have words given unto them many times, which confound the wise and the learned.

ALMA 32:23

On that early spring morning in 1820 when the light of truth and revelation dispelled the gloom of apostasy and confusion, a young boy was given a divine and gracious introduction and invitation: "This is My Beloved Son. Hear Him!" (JS—H 1:17). We may not each have the privilege of a personal visitation; nevertheless, these words are as personal an invitation to each of us as they were to the Prophet Joseph Smith—an invitation that carries with it an obligation to act on what we hear.

And how do we hear Him? We hear Him through the still small voice of inspiration, through the promised promptings of the Holy Ghost, through the voices of prophets of old who speak to us from the pages of the scriptures, through the voice of a living prophet who calls us his friends and bids us to draw near unto Christ by choosing to walk in His footsteps, and through the voice of the Savior Himself as we search the scriptures.

The most wondrous thing about this personal invitation is that it is neither age- nor gender-specific. During the Savior's ministry to the Nephites, little children listened, then "even babes did open their mouths and utter marvelous things" (3 Ne. 26:16) too sacred to be recorded.

> *A young boy emerged from a grove of trees after listening to a sacred message and spoke words that would forever change the course of mankind.*

In his boyhood, the Savior listened; then He confounded the learned men in the temple (see Luke 2:46–47). A young boy emerged from a grove of trees after listening to a sacred message and spoke words that would forever change the course of mankind (see JS—H). A faithful queen listened; then she trusted in God to save her people (see Esther 9). And children of God throughout the world hear Him and act on His words in wondrous ways.

❧

"I will tell you in your mind and in your heart, by the Holy Ghost, which shall come upon you and which shall dwell in your heart" (D&C 8:2).

GIFTS OF GOD

And again, I exhort you, my brethren, that ye deny not the gifts of God, for they are many; and they come from the same God. And there are different ways that these gifts are administered; but is the same God who worketh in all; and they are given by the manifestations of the Spirit of God unto men, to profit them. . . . And I would exhort you, my beloved brethren, that ye remember that every good gift cometh of Christ.

MORONI 10:8, 18

Both ancient and modern scriptures teach us that we are all blessed with gifts, which in turn bless the lives of others. "And all these gifts come from God, for the benefit of the children of God" (D&C 46:26). These gifts are as numerous and diverse as are all of God's children. When we look at the more obvious gifts—the gift of music, of speaking, of miracles, of tongues, of wisdom and knowledge, of faith, of healing—we may be tempted to wonder whether our gifts are significant or worthy of praise or mention.

The Savior's words reassure us that all gifts are praise-worthy and significant, because of the source from which they come: "For all have not every gift given unto them; for there are many gifts, and to every man is given a gift by the Spirit of God" (D&C 46:11). To be a good listener; to be patient in suffering; to find joy in service; to be discerning in our choices; to be strong in our testimony; to make our homes a haven where others feel safe and welcome; to enjoy the beauties of the earth; to enjoy the gifts and accomplishments of others; to contribute to the development of others' gifts, whether they be our family or our friends; to know how to touch and comfort, teach, and bless—these are all good gifts, and the Apostle Paul admonishes us to "Neglect not the gift that is in thee" (1 Tim. 4:14).

Never think that you have no gift to enjoy and share. God will tell us what our gifts are as we earnestly petition Him, and He will guide us in de-

> *Never think that you have no gift to enjoy and share.*

veloping and using them to bless our own lives and the lives of those with whom we associate.

Elder Marvin J. Ashton gave us wise and reassuring counsel when he reminded us that we sell ourselves short when we measure our gifts according to external standards such as social standing, physical appearance, or intellectual status. We all have God-given gifts, which we must recognize, develop, and use wisely (see "There Are Many Gifts," *Ensign*, Nov. 1987).

"If there is anything virtuous, lovely, or of good report or praiseworthy, we seek after these things" (A of F 1:13).

⁊

"Now there are diversities of gifts, but the same Spirit"
(1 Cor. 12:4).

Finding Favor with God

Behold, the Lord esteemeth all flesh in one; he that is righteous is favored of God.

1 Ne. 17:35

We are keenly aware of our daily need for food and water to sustain our physical bodies. Are we as concerned with sustenance for our spirits? As the Savior conversed with the Samaritan woman at the well, He taught her that while our physical hunger and thirst need constant satisfaction, "Whosoever drinketh of the water that I shall give him shall never thirst; but the water that I shall give him shall be in him a well of water springing up into everlasting life" (John 4: 14). He then expanded this metaphor when He taught, "For the bread of God is he which cometh down from heaven, and giveth life unto the world. . . . I am the bread of life: he that cometh to me shall never hunger" (John 6:33, 35).

We are all children at the well, needing that "water" of which the Savior speaks. And what *is* that "water"? It is the word of God that refreshes, revitalizes, and renews our drooping spirits. It is the gospel of Jesus Christ, the iron rod of saving principles and ordinances that guides us past the large and spacious buildings of the world. It is pure and clear and eternal, free from the contamination of deceit and fleeting pleasures. And just as the Savior gave life-sustaining manna to the children of Israel as they wandered in the wilderness, so He promises us spiritual nourishment that will sustain us in whatever "wilderness" we may be called on to traverse.

In His sermon to the Nephites, the Savior issues a benevolent invitation with the words, "Blessed are all they who do hunger and thirst after righteousness" (3 Ne 12:6). And what is the promise to all who accept this invitation and gather at His well of righteousness? We "shall be filled with the Holy Ghost" (3 Ne. 12:6), through whose ministrations we will be taught, enlightened, comforted, and led to a greater love for our Savior. Surely this is a promise and a gift worth claiming. As we embrace righteousness, we in turn are embraced by God's favor.

> *As we embrace righteousness, we in turn are embraced by God's favor.*

❧

President Dieter F. Uchtdorf counsels us that as we gain a greater knowledge of Christ's message, we as His disciples will be filled with a greater desire to emulate His life and teachings (see "The Way of the Disciple," Ensign, May 2009, 76).

The Lord's Book of Life

For the names of the righteous shall be written in the book of life, and unto them will I grant an inheritance at my right hand.

Alma 5:58

We increase in righteousness as we increase in love for one another. And as we increase in love for one another, we increase in love for God and His Beloved Son.

A simple yet powerful poem written by James Henry Leigh Hunt many years ago and one committed to memory by countless school children over the ages reminds us of one of the sure ways to know that our names will be numbered among the righteous, worthy of mention in the Book of Life:

Abou Ben Adhem (may his tribe increase!)
Awoke one night from a deep dream of peace,
And saw, within the moonlight of his room,
Making it rich, and like a lily in bloom,
An angel writing in a book of gold:—
Exceeding peace had made Ben Adhem bold,
And to the Presence in the room he said
"What writest thou?—The vision raised its head,
And with a look made of all sweet accord,
Answered, "The names of those who love the Lord."
"And is mine One?" said Abou. "Nay, not so,"

Replied the angel. Abou spoke more low,
But cheerily still, and said, "I pray thee, then,
Write me as one that loves his fellow men."
The angel wrote, and vanished. The next night
It came again with a great wakening light,
And showed the names of those whom love of God had blessed,
And lo! Ben Adhem's name led all the rest.

To receive honorable mention in the Lord's Book of Life is most assuredly an

> We increase in righteousness as we increase in love for one another. And as we increase in love for one another, we increase in love for God and His Beloved Son.

indication of the promise of an eternal and celestial inheritance for the righteous. The Psalmist declares: "The Lord knoweth the days of the upright: and their inheritance shall be for ever" (Ps. 37:18).

✤

Speaking of those who are eligible for an eternal and celestial inheritance, the Lord says, "These are they whose names are written in heaven, where God and Christ are the judge of all" (D&C 76:68).

GRATITUDE

And behold also, if I, whom ye call your king, who has spent his days in your service, and yet has been in the service of God, do merit any thanks from you, O how you ought to thank your heavenly King!

MOSIAH 2:19

On the occasion of the Last Supper, Jesus both served and instructed His Apostles. In so doing, He expressed His gratitude and love for them and continued to do so in His great intercessory prayer, once again setting the pattern and example for the attitude of gratitude we should cultivate.

We read in the Doctrine and Covenants, "Thou shalt thank the Lord thy God in all things" (D&C 59:7). A simple yet profound children's song reiterates this admonition beautifully:

> I thank thee, dear Father in heaven above,
> For thy goodness and mercy, thy kindness and love.
> I thank thee for home, friends, and parents so dear,
> And for ev'ry blessing that I enjoy here (CSB, 7).

Elder Henry B. Eyring challenges us to make "thank you" a priority in our prayers. He explains that verbal expressions of gratitude increase our recollections of blessings received, making our prayers more heartfelt and less rushed (see *To Draw Closer to God* [Salt Lake City: Deseret Book, 1997], 78).

It is good to be grateful in times of need and turmoil as well as in times of personal peace and plenty. Following a hospital visit to a son who was dying of cancer, a grieving mother encountered a neighbor whose husband had also been diagnosed with this terminal disease, and whose remaining days were few. As these women embraced and shed tears together, the wise and insightful neighbor made the following observation: "Aren't we blessed to have had the sweet association of these loved ones for as long as we did?" In the midst of sorrow and impending loss, this simple expression of gratitude brought a measure of peace and comfort and a reason to rejoice.

The Psalmist tell us that "It is a good thing to give thanks unto the Lord" (Ps. 92:1). Let us be grateful

It is good to be grateful in times of need and turmoil as well as in times of personal peace and plenty.

children of God, at all times and in all circumstances. Let us joyfully count our blessings and "name them one by one" (*Hymns*, no. 241). Let us "live in thanksgiving daily, for the many mercies and blessings which he doth bestow upon [us]" (Alma 34:38). Let us remember with gratitude that the world is glorious, truth has been restored, and God lives and loves us.

ॐ

"And he who receiveth all things with thankfulness shall be made glorious; and the things of this earth shall be added unto him, even an hundred fold, yea, more"
(D&C 78:19).

RESURRECTION—A GIFT FOR ALL

The soul shall be restored to the body, and the body to the soul; yea, and every limb and joint shall be restored to its body; yea, even a hair of the head shall not be lost; but all things shall be restored to their proper and perfect frame. . . . And then shall the righteous shine forth in the kingdom of God.

ALMA 40:23, 25

Following the Savior's Resurrection, Mary Magdalene stood at the door of the empty sepulchre weeping, supposing that someone had removed His body to another place. The risen Lord spoke to her saying, "Woman, why weepest thou? Whom seekest thou?" (John 20:15). Inexplicable joy replaced Mary's sorrow as the eyes of her understanding were opened and she recognized the Savior—and comprehended the reality of His Resurrection.

Just as Mary Magdalene wept and wondered on the whereabouts of her beloved Lord, sometimes we question in our pain-filled moments, "Where art thou?" (D&C 121:1). Then from a loving Heavenly Father comes the quiet but powerful assurance that the Savior lives—that He is indeed the risen Lord, whose love can lift and comfort our sorrowing spirits, renew our faltering faith, and bring joy and peace and hope to our souls.

"For behold, this is my work and my glory—to bring to pass the immortality and eternal life of man" (Moses 1:39). This scripture not only reminds us of the promise and precious privilege of resurrection and the Lord's desire to have us share in His exaltation, but it also carries the gentle message that He finds joy in offering this gift—He glories in being our Savior.

He wants us to succeed. He wants us to be ever mindful of His love, of His outstretched and comforting arms, of His awareness of our needs.

The prophet Alma assured his son regarding the reality of the resurrection: "The soul shall be restored to the body, and the body to the soul; yea, and every limb and joint shall be restored to its body; yea, even a hair of the head shall not be lost; but all things shall be restored to their proper and perfect frame" (Alma 40:43).

Prophets of God in all dispensations have testified boldly of the Savior's Resurrection. In the dispensation of the fulness of times, the Prophet Joseph Smith's magnificent testimony echoes all these ancient prophetic affirmations:

> *Prophets of God in all dispensations have testified boldly of the Savior's Resurrection.*

"And now, after the many testimonies which have been given of him, this is the testimony, last of all, which we give of him: That he lives!" (D&C 76:22). And all succeeding prophets in this dispensation have testified with this same unwavering conviction that Jesus Christ is indeed our living Savior and Redeemer (see "He Lives! The Witness of Latter-day Prophets," *Ensign*, Mar. 2008, 8–11).

"Oh, sweet, the joy this sentence gives: 'I know that my Redeemer lives!'" (*Hymns*, no. 136).

✂

"For as in Adam all die, even so in Christ shall all be made alive" (1 Cor. 15:22).

19

THE SAVIOR'S EXAMPLE

. . . Behold I am the light; I have set an example for you.

3 NE. 18:16

When the Savior says, "come, follow me" (Luke 18:22), we know that heeding His words and actions will lead us in paths of righteousness because of His perfect example.

He sets for us the example of love and tender compassion in His admonition to love one another as He loves all of His children. The scriptures are replete with examples of those whom He loved: the woman at the well; the woman taken in adultery; the publican with whom He chose to have lunch; the lepers, the blind, the crippled, and the otherwise unfortunate ones He so graciously healed; those He raised from the dead; the multitudes He fed after a long and exhausting day of teaching and healing; the children He blessed—one by one—as He wept over them and prayed for them and encircled them with the fire of guardian angels. We read of His desire to gather and protect His children "even as a hen gathereth her chickens under her wings" (Matt. 23:37) and of His desire to find even one lost and straying lamb.

As the greatest of all Teachers, He sets for us the example of creativity and enthusiasm. For where He went, crowds always followed—in the heat of the day, on storm-tossed seas, and over rough terrains—because He taught with dignity and intensity based on His own careful preparation and humility, which in turn led to greater knowledge He could share with His followers. His parables are both simple and profound, and as we listen to and study His words, we have "eyes to see, and ears to hear" (Deut. 29:4) great lessons and truths: prayer and devotion to the gospel; forgiveness for ourselves and others; an enthusiastic defense of righteous principles and a vigorous denunciation of ungodly practices; and the wisdom of balancing the letter and the spirit of the law, to name just a few.

> *His example is indeed the "light [that] shineth in darkness" (John 1:5), the Light that gives meaning and direction to our lives.*

The Savior's example is indeed the "light [that] shineth in darkness" (John 1:5), the Light that gives meaning and direction to our lives. The Psalmist declares, "Thy word is a lamp unto my feet, and a light unto my path" (Ps. 119:105). How grateful we are for our Savior's supreme example, for His loving willingness to light our way and guide our footsteps.

"For I have given you an example, that ye should do as I have done to you" (John 13:15).

Our Savior's Love

Behold, I have graven thee upon the palms of my hands; thy walls are continually before me.

1 NE. 21:16

The Savior's sacrifice and suffering both in Gethsemane and on Calvary were motivated by love, and His scars are testaments of that love—vivid yet tender reminders to both Jew and Gentile alike that "God so loved the world, that he gave his only begotten Son, that whosoever believeth in him should not perish, but have everlasting life" (John 3:16).

The Savior's scars remind us that we are saved in a very real and eternal sense only by and through His redeeming grace. They are the wounds "with which [he] was wounded in the house of [his] friends" (Zech. 13:6), yet they are the very wounds with which "He healeth the broken in heart, and bindeth up their wounds" (Ps. 147:3)—with which He will wipe away all tears (see Rev. 20:4).

When the Savior visited the Nephites sometime after His Crucifixion and Resurrection, He invited a multitude of 2,500 people to feel the wounds in His hands, feet, and side. What a glorious experience that must have been. And the Savior's invitation intended that this experience would be personal and tender for each one of those people—men, women, and children.

"And this they did do, going forth one by one until they had all gone forth, and did see with their eyes and did feel with their hands, and did know of a surety and did bear record, that it was he, of whom it was written by the prophets, that should come. And when they had all gone forth and had witnessed for themselves, they did cry out with one record, saying: Hosanna! Blessed be the name of the Most High God! And they did fall down at the feet of Jesus, and did worship him" (3 Ne. 11:15–17).

Can you imagine the joy of all the Book of Mormon prophets as they saw prophecy fulfilled—as they saw their children at long last knowing and indeed seeing the source of the remission of their sins? One of our Primary songs says it so well: "I should like to have been with Him then" (CSB, 56).

However, the Savior extends that same invitation to each one of us. Elder Jeffrey R. Holland expresses it quite beautifully. He says, in essence, that the Savior extends His hands to us in a warm invitation to come unto Him, to feel His healing touch in our lives, to know that His love is sure and constant (see "Broken Things to Mend," *Ensign*, May 2006).

> *The Savior's sacrifice and suffering both in Gethsemane and on Calvary were motivated by love.*

The Savior Himself offers these comforting words: "Behold, I have graven thee upon the palms of my hands" (Isa. 49:16).

❧

"Behold the wounds which pierced my side, and also the prints of the nails in my hands and feet; be faithful, keep my commandments, and ye shall inherit the kingdom of heaven. Amen"
(D&C 6:37).

13 Repentance

And it came to pass that I, Nephi, did exhort my brethren, with all diligence, to keep the commandments of the Lord. And it came to pass that they did humble themselves before the Lord; insomuch that I had joy and great hopes of them, that they would walk in the paths of righteousness.

1 Ne. 16:4–5

Nephi joyously recognized his brothers' humility, knowing that it was certainly the first step in the right direction toward repentance and walking in paths of righteousness. President Gordon B. Hinckley assured us that if we lay aside our pride and arrogance, then surely the Lord will keep His promise to lead us as He hears and answers prayers (see "A Prophet's Prayer and Counsel for Youth," *Ensign*, Jan. 2001, 2).

Being led by the Lord surely means walking in paths of righteousness. Parents of small children understand how important it is to lead them by the hand in order to protect them from the dangers of crossing busy streets or becoming lost in large crowds. Sometimes, in their eagerness to assert their independence, our children resist this guidance, but a wise parent knows the importance of persisting in and insisting on this practice, for therein lies safety.

In much the same way, the Savior desires to take our hand in order to ensure our spiritual safety.

Sometimes we resist this guidance, thinking that surely we are old enough and big enough to manage on our own. The words of one of our much-loved scriptures provide a powerful antidote for this type of thinking: "Be thou humble; and the Lord thy God shall lead thee by the hand, and give thee answer to thy prayers" (D&C 112:10).

True repentance requires us to truly humble ourselves and seek the Lord's help and forgiveness. We draw comfort and encouragement from the words of King Benjamin: "And again, believe that ye must repent of your sins and forsake them, and humble yourselves before God; and ask in sincerity of heart that he would forgive you" (Mosiah 4:10).

President Spencer W. Kimball tells us how eager the Lord is to reach out to us as we humbly seek His help in our repentance process, making it possible to accomplish all the righteous desires of our hearts. He reminds us that we are reliant on the Lord as we seek to change our lives. By ourselves, we fall short, but with the Lord's help we can accomplish anything we desire to do, regardless of the enormity of the task (see *The Miracle of Forgiveness* [Salt Lake City: Bookcraft, 1969], 176).

> *"Be thou humble; and the Lord thy God shall lead thee by the hand, and give thee answer to thy prayers" (D&C 112:10).*

❦

When we humble ourselves before the Lord, we acknowledge our weakness and our dependence on Him. This is the first step on the path to repentance and signals our faith in His atoning love.

TEMPLE WORSHIP

And many people shall go and say, Come ye, and let us go up to the mountain of the Lord, to the house of the God of Jacob; and he will teach us of his ways, and we will walk in his paths; for out of Zion shall go forth the law, and the word of the Lord from Jerusalem.

2 NE. 12:3

Temple attendance is a sacred, "mountaintop" experience and privilege. There, as the prophet Isaiah foretold, we are taught the doctrines of the kingdom and we learn how to walk in the Lord's paths.

The temple is a house of prayer and instruction. It is a house of inspiration and revelation unlike any other place on earth. Prayers are answered there; guidance is given, and windows of wisdom are opened up. Every time we attend the temple we are enriched by new insights; gospel doctrines take on added meanings.

The temple is the means for the perpetuation of eternal relationships. The eternal family is the basis of the gospel of Jesus Christ, and the promise of eternal relationships is at the heart of our temple attendance and worship.

The temple is a place of safety and protection, of peace and comfort. The temple offers refuge and protection from the onslaught of temptation and moral decadence so common in our society today. In the temple, one has a sense of the protecting hand of God extended in love and compassion.

The temple is a house of service. There is no other place where we can avail ourselves of the sacred opportunity to be engaged in a work that reaches beyond the veil of mortality and into the eternities.

In the Doctrine and Covenants, the Prophet Joseph Smith affirms the joy of service on behalf of those who have gone before us: "Let your hearts rejoice, and be exceedingly glad. Let the earth break forth into singing. Let the dead speak forth anthems of eternal praise to the King Immanuel, who hath ordained, before the world was, that which would enable us to redeem them out of their prison; for the prisoners shall go free. . . . Let us, therefore, as a church and a people, and as Latter-day Saints, offer unto the Lord an offering in righteousness; and let us present in his holy temple, when it is finished, a book containing the records of our dead, which shall be worthy of all acceptation" (D&C 128:22, 24).

> *Every time we attend the temple we are enriched by new insights; gospel doctrines take on added meanings.*

The ultimate destiny of the faithful children of God is to dwell forever in His presence in a state of everlasting glory as an eternal family, and in the temple we are clearly and lovingly instructed as to how we can fulfill this celestial mission.

❧

"One thing I have desired of the Lord, that I will seek after; that I may dwell in the house of the Lord all the days of my life, to behold the beauty of the Lord, and to enquire in his temple"
(Ps. 27:4).

TRUST IN JESUS

O Lord, I have trusted in thee, and I will trust in thee forever. I will not put my trust in the arm of flesh; for I know that cursed is he that putteth his trust in the arm of flesh. Yea, cursed is he that putteth his trust in man or maketh flesh his arm.

2 Ne. 4: 34

Nephi's psalm is both powerful and poignant. We are deeply moved by his soul-searching words, by his confession of spiritual weakness, by his expressions of gratitude for the many blessings and tender mercies of the Lord, by his unshakable testimony of Christ. When we consider the numerous trials he endured, including the hateful and murderous actions of his own brothers, his unwavering example of faith and trust in the Lord is nothing short of stunning.

In a world of voices and forces that would have us live in fear and trembling of "the arm of man" and what it can do, how blessed we are to know where we can turn for peace and safety. "The Lord is my light and my salvation; whom then shall I fear? The Lord is the strength of my life; of whom shall I be afraid?" (Ps. 27:1). Tenderly the Savior tells us, "Fear not, little children, for you are mine" (D&C 50:41).

Elder Jeffrey R. Holland acknowledges that no one is exempt from affliction in all its varying forms; that is just one of mortality's realities. However, as we put our trust in Jesus, we will find the strength to go forward with faith (see *Trusting Jesus* [Salt Lake City: Deseret Book, 2003]).

Just as in the days of the Prophet Joseph Smith, we hear the cries all around us of "Lo, here!" and "Lo, there!"—voices that entice us to walk in ungodly paths, that attempt to intimidate us as we cling to the iron rod and "press forward with a steadfastness in Christ . . . feasting upon the word of Christ" (2 Ne. 31:20). Those voices tell us that the here and now is all that counts, that society's approval far outweighs the Savior's approbation. How comforting it is to know that we can rely on our Savior's love, guidance, and protection.

As we put our trust in the arm of the Lord, we can

> *In a world of voices and forces that would have us live in fear and trembling of "the arm of man" and what it can do, how blessed we are to know where we can turn for peace and safety.*

joyfully and confidently proclaim like Nephi of old: "We talk of Christ, we rejoice in Christ . . ." (2 Ne. 25:26). We will understand, like the Psalmist expresses in Psalm 23:1–6, that the Lord is our shepherd who "leadeth [us] in the paths of righteousness . . . whose goodness and mercy will follow [us] all the days of [our lives]" until we return safely to His presence.

"Blessed is the man that trusteth in the Lord, and whose hope the Lord is" (Jer. 17:7).

A Parent's Stewardship

And ye will not suffer your children that they go hungry, or naked; neither will ye suffer that they transgress the laws of God, and fight and quarrel one with another, and serve the devil. . . . But ye will teach them to walk in the ways of truth and soberness; ye will teach them to love one another, and to serve one another.

MOSIAH 4:14–15

President David O. McKay taught that "no other success can compensate for failure in the home" (*Improvement Era*, June 1964, 445), a doctrine later emphasized by President Harold B. Lee when he reminded us that the greatest work we as parents do will be within the walls of our own homes (see *Ensign*, July 1973, 98). In his closing remarks of the October 2000 General Conference of the Church, President Gordon B. Hinckley offered his own gentle admonition to parents to speak softly and use the language of love in our homes.

The love of parents inspires love among their children. The influence of righteous parents in the home is unrivaled as it sets the tone for relationships, interactions, and instruction. King Benjamin spoke of this plainly to the parents in his congregation as he gathered them together to hear words of inspiration regarding the raising of their children. He said, "ye will teach them to love one another, and to serve one another" (Mosiah 4:15). Of course, the best teacher is example. Parents are naturally service-oriented, and their examples of selfless and loving service freely and joyfully performed are an inspiration to all those who dwell within the walls of their homes.

In "The Family: A Proclamation to the World," we are taught that the duty of parents is to guide and rear our children in all ways and in all things; to teach them obedience to God's laws and to the laws of the land.

Loving parents encourage happy interchanges and delight and share in the spiritual, social, and emotional growth of their children. They dare them to dream, to reach outward, to reach upward, and to revel in the happy

> The love of parents inspires love among their children. The influence of righteous parents in the home is unrivaled as it sets the tone for relationships, interactions, and instruction.

safety of their home. They understand and believe that "The light of faith abides within the heart of every child" (*Hymns*, no. 305) as they carefully nurture that faith so that it will grandly grow into an independent entity. They happily join the prophet Moroni in saying, "I love little children with a perfect love" (Moro. 8:17).

❧

It should be the right of every child to be able to say, as did Nephi, that they have been "born of goodly parents" (1 Ne. 1:1).

A SURE FOUNDATION

And now, my sons, remember, remember that it is upon the rock of our Redeemer, who is Christ, the Son of God, that ye must build your foundation; that when the devil shall send forth his mighty winds, yea, his shafts in the whirlwind, yea, when all his hail and his mighty storm shall beat upon you, it shall have no power over you to drag you down to the gulf of endless misery and endless wo, because of the rock upon which ye are built, which is a sure foundation, a foundation whereon if men build they cannot fall.

HEL. 5:12

In a world where we are beset by an increasing crescendo of natural disasters, where financial stability is sometimes fleeting and elusive, where the media is often fascinated and fixated on that which is sensational rather than that which is rational, we might be tempted to ask ourselves this question: Is there anything or anyone we can truly trust? Helaman's words spoken to his sons and to all who will read and heed them reassure us that there is "safety for the soul" (*Hymns*, no. 239).

The Savior tells us that He is "the way, the truth, and the life" (John 14:6); that He is "the light of the world" (John 8:12). And therein lies the simple yet grand answer to our question. It is Christ in whom we put our trust, for as Helaman reminds us, He is a sure foundation, a mighty Rock.

When we consider the natural disasters that are becoming ever more frequent, we see that the construction industry is becoming increasingly conscious of building codes that endeavor to guarantee some measure of stability to homes and other buildings should these disasters strike. There are, however, no 100 percent guarantees against the forces of nature, and builders and homeowners alike always fear the worst. Contrast that with the Lord's promise regarding His spiritual foundation. No forces of earth and hell combined can prevail against it, and we are free from the fear of defeat or downfall. Therein lies the 100 percent guarantee.

> *It is Christ in whom we put our trust, for as Helaman reminds us, He is a sure foundation, a mighty Rock.*

And again the Savior Himself reminds us of His promise to those who build their lives on His sure foundation: "Fear thou not; for I am with thee: be not dismayed; for I am thy God: I will strengthen thee; yea, I will help thee; yea, I will uphold thee with the right hand of my righteousness" (Isa. 41:10).

❧

"Therefore, fear not, little flock; do good; let earth and hell combine against you, for if ye are built upon my rock, they cannot prevail" (D&C 6:34).

THE LORD'S TENDER MERCIES 18

But behold, I, Nephi, will show unto you that the tender mercies of the Lord are over all those whom he hath chosen, because of their faith, to make them mighty even unto the power of deliverance.

1 NE. 1:20

Nephi's words evoke powerful images and carry with them a comforting promise to all who are faithful. *Mercy* is defined as a divine favor or an act of compassion. Elder David A. Bednar explains that the Lord's *tender mercies* are very often private and personal blessings from a loving Savior who knows our needs, who is anxious to lend His strength and His support, and who wants to bestow upon us the spiritual gifts that are beneficial for us personally. Elder Bednar further explains that some of the Lord's tender mercies include the gifts of faith, repentance, forgiveness, persistence, and fortitude (see "The Tender Mercies of the Lord," *Ensign*, May 2005, 99).

And on whom does the Lord choose to bestow these tender mercies? Nephi tells us that through our faith—faith in the Lord Jesus Christ, faith in His great atoning sacrifice, faith in His unconditional love for all of His children, faith that leads us to love and serve Him diligently in whatever opportunities we might be given—we can be chosen to receive these great and tender blessings.

Certainly the word *tender* is well and wisely chosen. It evokes images of the loving-kindnesses of which Elder Bednar speaks. As we examine our relationship with the Lord, surely we are reminded of tender mercies that are most often quiet and personal—a kind and encouraging word spoken when our heart is heavy, a quiet act of service that lightens our load and reminds us that we are loved and

> *As we examine our relationship with the Lord, we are reminded of tender mercies that are most often quiet and personal.*

remembered, a smile from a stranger that brightens our day, a sincere compliment that tells us that we are worthwhile and important. These are the tender and heavenly-inspired mercies that have the power to deliver us from the burdens that beset us all from time to time.

Well might we ponder the words of the Psalmist: "I trust in the mercy of God for ever and ever" (Ps. 52:8). Such trust will never be misplaced, and will surely be rewarded.

"Thy mercy, Lord, is great
And far above the heav'ns.
Let none be made ashamed
That wait upon thee" (Hymns, no. 110).

A Mighty Change of Heart

And now behold, I ask of you, my brethren of the church, have ye spiritually been born of God? Have ye received his image in your countenances? Have ye experienced this mighty change in your hearts?

ALMA 5:14

Alma the Younger asks three crucial questions in this scripture. If anyone knew from personal experience the importance of these questions and the need to be able to answer them in the affirmative, it was most certainly this revered prophet of God. His conversion from a zealous apostate to that of a stalwart and mighty missionary was truly miraculous. Upon regaining his strength after being struck down by an angel, he knew what it was to be spiritually born of God and clearly explains the process for all of us. We must be "changed from their carnal and fallen state, to a state of righteousness, being redeemed of God" (Mosiah 27:25), thus becoming worthy to inherit the kingdom of God.

As worthy sons and daughters of God, our countenances reflect that divine relationship; we reflect His light that He so generously shares with us, and that light is in turn reflected in our every thought, word, and deed.

And what is the mighty change of heart? It is a disposition to do what is right, having faith in Christ and His Atonement; in other words, it is a desire to repent and come unto Christ. King Lamoni was willing to exchange his kingdom for this changed heart; Paul gladly endured persecution, pain, and poverty once his heart was changed, and he had no more desire to do evil.

President Ezra Taft Benson explained that after King Benjamin concluded his inspiring address in the land of Zarahemla, the people were united in their belief on his words: "And they all cried with one voice, saying: Yea, we believe all the words which thou hast spoken unto us; and also, we know of their surety and truth, because of the Spirit of the Lord Omnipotent, which has wrought a might change in us, or in our hearts, that we have no more disposition to do evil, but to do good continually" (Mosiah 5:2). President Benson went on to say that as we experience this same mighty change through our faith in Jesus Christ and through the witness of the Spirit, we become a new person.

> *When we have undergone this mighty change, which is brought about only through faith in Jesus Christ and through the operation of the Spirit upon us, it is as though we have become a new person.*

A mighty change of heart is like a new birth (see "A Mighty Change of Heart," *Ensign*, Oct. 1989, 2).

We must carefully preserve this mighty change of heart. It would be well to frequently ask ourselves Alma's follow-up question: "If ye have experienced a change of heart, and if ye have felt to sing the song of redeeming love, I would ask, can ye feel so now?" (Alma 5:26).

"For as he thinketh in his heart, so is he" (Prov. 23:7).

RIGHTEOUS MOTHERS

Now they had never fought, yet they did not fear death; and they did think more upon the liberty of their fathers than they did upon their lives; yea, they had been taught by their mothers, that if they did not doubt, God would deliver them. And they rehearsed unto me the words of their mothers, saying: We do not doubt our mothers knew it.

ALMA 56:47–48

These words spoken by the stripling warriors as they prepared to go into battle are a fitting tribute to their mothers, whose examples of faith and fidelity to gospel principles had a profound influence and effect on these young men. Herein we see the power of a mother's love and the teaching of correct principles.

President Gordon B. Hinckley said that the influence of righteous mothers is mirrored in a nation's strength. As mothers quietly and consistently teach their children basic values, those teachings will be reflected in their children's characters and in the society in which they live (see *Teachings of Gordon B. Hinckley* [Salt Lake City: Deseret Book, 1997], 386).

Motherhood is a sweet and tender stewardship bestowed by Heavenly Father, who knows a woman's heart. It is a partnership with God, whose greatest desire is to have His children return to live with Him. A daunting yet delightful experience, motherhood carries with it the responsibility to teach, train, admonish, nurture, encourage, protect, love, and, above all, to take delight in knowing that "Children are an heritage of the Lord" (Ps. 127:3).

> *Motherhood is a sweet and tender stewardship bestowed by Heavenly Father, who knows a woman's heart.*

We find in Psalms 113:9 a lovely reminder to "be a joyful mother of children." With all the responsibilities that come with our calling as mothers, we need to take time to rejoice in the small and daily moments of joy that are attendant with each precious child, at all ages and stages of their lives.

Mormon tells us, "Little children are alive in Christ" (Moro. 8:12). This knowledge and promise encourage and motivate us to love, enjoy, and expend our every effort to return these precious charges back to the presence of a Father and Savior who eagerly await their homecoming.

"Of such is the kingdom of God" (Luke 18:16).

21

CHARITY

But charity is the pure love of Christ, and it endureth forever; and whoso is possessed of it at the last day, it shall be well with him.

MORO. 7:47

In this scripture we are taught three rather magnificent truths about charity. First, it is the pure love of Christ—which is, as the Bible Dictionary tells us, the highest, noblest, and strongest kind of love. It is love that looks beyond outward appearances and sees the intent and goodness of others' hearts. It is love that is not judgmental. It is love that encourages the recipients to do their best without measuring that "best" against the accomplishments of others. It is the love shown by the Savior throughout His mortal ministry and manifest in countless quiet and sometimes even spectacular ways in our daily lives. Charity is the love that we have for our Heavenly Father and our Savior, which in turn transforms itself into love for our fellowmen. "Beloved, let us love one another: for love is of God; and every one that loveth is born of God, and knoweth God" (1 Jn. 4:7).

Second, it endures forever. It is not a fleeting or capricious emotion, but one that can be counted on at all times and in all situations. It is motivated by the Savior's example of unconditional and enduring love—a love that motivated His great atoning sacrifice in our behalf, the effects of which are eternal. President Ezra Taft Benson added to Mormon's definition of charity by explaining that the pure love of Christ is far removed from the world's concept of love. It is selfless love, motivated by a desire to help our fellow men experience the joy of spiritual growth (see *Ensign*, Nov. 1986, 47).

Third, we learn that it will be well with anyone who is possessed of this attribute at the last day. This is a gentle and lovely understatement of a divine promise of eternal life. As with any good habit or character trait, charity is not a last-minute acquisition; it is a trait to be cultivated and nurtured and practiced on a daily basis, so that when that "last day" comes, it is firmly in place.

> *Charity is the love that we have for our Heavenly Father and our Savior, which in turn transforms itself into love for our fellowmen.*

On the occasion of the Last Supper, the Savior gave a new commandment to His Apostles. "A new commandment I give unto you, That ye love one another; as I have loved you, that ye also love one another" (John 13:34). This can leave no doubt in our minds regarding the priority that the pure love of Christ should have in our lives, both as we receive it and practice it.

"He that loveth not knoweth not God; for God is love"
(1 Jn. 4:8).

Salvation Comes through Christ

And now, my brethren, I have spoken plainly that ye cannot err. And as the Lord God liveth that brought Israel up out of the land of Egypt, and gave unto Moses power that he should heal the nations after they had been bitten by the poisonous serpents, if they would cast their eyes unto the serpent which he did raise up before them, and also gave him power that he should smite the rock and the water should come forth; yea, behold I say unto you, that as these things are true, and as the Lord God liveth, there is none other name given under heaven save it be this Jesus Christ, of which I have spoken, whereby man can be saved.

2 Ne. 25:20

It is always somewhat exciting to be able to claim a connection to a famous person, whether that person belongs to the world of sports, entertainment, an institution of higher learning, or some other prestigious organization. In so doing, we are sometimes labeled as "name droppers," a label that is not necessarily complimentary. And the famous person usually has little regard for our admiration and even less respect for our claim of mutual association.

There is, however, a name with which all of us can safely and proudly claim a connection—the name of Jesus Christ. He is our claim to eternal fame. To put it in more reverent terms, He is our promise of eternal life, someone through whom we can enjoy the companionship of both Father and Son. "For God so loved the world, that he gave his only begotten Son, that whosoever believeth in him should not perish, but have everlasting life" (John 3:16).

The scriptures make it abundantly clear that the Savior is the only name through which this promise can be claimed, and it is a doctrine known well by prophets in all dispensations. This sacred truth was given to Enoch, to whom the Father testified that Jesus Christ was "the only name which shall be given under heaven, whereby salvation shall come unto the children of men" (Moses 6:52). It was reiterated by that great Apostle Peter, who testified that "there is none other name under heaven given among men, whereby we must be saved" (Acts 4:12). And in the dispensation of the fulness of times, the Lord revealed through the Prophet Joseph Smith that "Jesus Christ is the name which is given of the Father, and there is none other name given whereby man can be saved" (D&C 18:23).

> *How glorious it is to know that our Savior knows us and loves us and welcomes our association with His sacred name. How blessed we are to claim the privilege of knowing Him.*

How glorious it is to know that our Savior knows us and loves us and welcomes our association with His sacred name. How blessed we are to claim the privilege of knowing Him.

*"Jesus, the very thought of thee
With sweetness fills my breast;
But sweeter far thy face to see
And in thy presence rest"* (Hymns, no. 141).

THE LORD'S LOVE FOR LITTLE CHILDREN

And he spake unto the multitude, and said unto them: Behold your little ones. And as they looked to behold they cast their eyes towards heaven, and they saw the heavens open, and they saw angels descending out of heaven as if it were in the midst of fire; and they came down and encircled those little ones about, and they were encircled about with fire; and the angels did minister unto them.

3 NE. 17:23–24

The Savior's love for little children is recorded throughout the scriptures. He expressed these tender feelings through words and deeds, and nowhere are words and deeds more lovely than when He ministered on the American continent among the Nephites. After healing those people who were afflicted with all manner of infirmities, the Savior wept with a fulness of joy, which joy only increased as He took the children and blessed them individually, invoking Heavenly Father's blessings upon them as well. Then he bade the entire congregation to behold their little ones.

Elder M. Russell Ballard offers a thoughtful insight to this sacred instruction. He points out that when the Savior used the word *behold*, He meant more than a cursory glance. The word carries with it a tender entreaty to love them and look inward to their God-given spirits, and treat them accordingly (see Church Fireside, broadcast from Salt Lake Tabernacle, Jan. 23, 1994).

In speaking of little children, the Savior reminds us all that "of such is the kingdom of God" (Luke 18:16). He teaches us that unless we "become as little children, [we] shall not enter into the kingdom of heaven" (Matt. 18:3).

The touching words in the song "Consider the Lilies" express the Lord's deep love and concern for His sweet, tender children, regardless where or when they live. Any pain or suffering they are called to endure was part of the Savior's bur-

> *In speaking of little children, the Savior reminds us all that "of such is the kingdom of God" (Luke 18:16).*

den of sorrow and suffering in the Garden of Gethsemane.

The angels who encircled the Nephite children and ministered to them provide a splendid example to parents of children everywhere. We are entrusted with the Lord's little ones, and it is our sacred duty to guide them safely back to His loving presence.

❧

As we consider the Savior's love for little children, it is comforting to think of ourselves as His little children as well. Our heavenly parentage and our earthly stewardships are inseparably connected. "Fear not, little children, for you are mine, and I have overcome the world, and you are of them that my Father hath given me" (D&C 50:41).

Spiritual Cleanliness

And may the Lord bless you, and keep your garments spotless, that ye may at last be brought to sit down with Abraham, Isaac, and Jacob, and the holy prophets who have been ever since the world began, having your garments spotless even as their garments are spotless, in the kingdom of heaven to go no more out.

Alma 7:25

This scripture carries with it a plea for inner cleanliness. The Savior frequently referred to the need for inner integrity, especially when dealing with the Pharisees of His day. In fact, He likened the lack of inner cleanliness to a "whited sepulchre," a phrase denoting an outward appearance that belied the corruption within. The Lord also used another metaphor when denouncing the hypocrisy of the Pharisees: "Now do ye Pharisees make clean the outside of the cup and the platter; but your inward part is full of ravening and wickedness" (Luke 11:39).

In Joseph Smith's day, the Savior illustrated such a dichotomy when speaking of those whose professions of godliness are nothing but empty rhetoric: "They draw near to me with their lips, but their hearts are far from me" (JS—H 1:19). These words carry a timely caution for all of us. It is possible but not admirable for us to be pennies passing ourselves off as silver dollars.

The term "spotless garments" implies that we are clean inside and out. Our thoughts, words, and actions mesh perfectly and consistently. We are on weekdays what we profess to be on Sundays. Our every action can withstand the closest scrutiny, and we can gladly and confidently "walk in the light." There is no fear of exposure that would bring shame or embarrassment to our families and friends. And most importantly, there is no hypocrisy that would disappoint the Lord and jeopardize our right to an inheritance in our Father's kingdom.

> *The term spotless garments implies that we are clean inside and out.*

The Psalmist asks the question, "Who shall ascend into the hill of the Lord? or who shall stand in his holy place?" (Ps. 24:3). Then comes the answer, and with it the accompanying promise: "He that hath clean hands, and a pure heart; who hath not lifted up his soul unto vanity, nor sworn deceitfully. He shall receive the blessing from the Lord, and righteousness from the God of his salvation" (Ps. 24:3–5).

We often think that "cleanliness is next to godliness" applies to personal and physical hygiene—but how much more aptly does it apply to our spotless spiritual garments?

"There can no man be saved except his garments are washed white; yea, his garments must be purified" (Alma 5:21).

God Loves All His Children

Now my brethren, we see that God is mindful of every people, whatsoever land they may be in; yea, he numbereth his people, and his bowels of mercy are over all the earth. Now this is my joy, and my great thanksgiving; yea, and I will give thanks unto my God forever. Amen.

ALMA 26:37

Heavenly Father knows each one of us by name, and He is constantly aware of our needs and our longings, our joys and our sorrows, our triumphs and temptations—indeed He is aware of the very intent of our heart.

He loves us and rejoices in our diversities, whether they are differences in race, color, height, weight, appearance, marital status, social standing, educational opportunities, or our physical, mental, and emotional needs. We are each valuable and important in the eyes of our Heavenly Father and His Son, even when we stumble, fall, or lose our way. Though we may not look or feel or act exactly like anyone else, They love us and accept us and see our potential and worth.

Nephi tells us, "And he inviteth them all to come unto him and partake of his goodness; and he denieth none that come unto him, black and white, bond and free, male and female; and he remembereth the heathen; and all are alike unto God, both Jew and Gentile" (2 Ne. 26:33).

While serving as a member of the Quorum of the Twelve, Elder Howard W. Hunter stated that we are all literally brothers and sisters, spirit children of our Heavenly Father. In our premortal state we were one large eternal family, and we enjoyed a familial relationship there. Our Heavenly Parents give us a common paternity as well as a literal brotherhood and sisterhood (see "All Are Alike unto God," *Ensign*, June 1979, 72).

How kind and gracious and wise is our Heavenly Father, who celebrates our differences and

> *Heavenly Father knows each one of us by name.*

exhorts us to do the same, so that we may learn to grow in love for one another as brothers and sisters, looking past outward appearances and inward toward the heart. "For the Lord looketh on the heart" (1 Sam. 19:7).

There is no one else quite like us. We should celebrate our uniqueness and our value in the eyes of God.

"But in every nation he that feareth him, and worketh righteousness, is accepted with him" (Acts 10:35).

FORMULA FOR ETERNAL LIFE

Wherefore, ye must press forward with a steadfastness in Christ, having a perfect brightness of hope, and a love of God and of all men. Wherefore, if ye shall press forward, feasting upon the words of Christ, and endure to the end, behold, thus saith the Father: Ye shall have eternal life.

2 NE. 31:20

The Savior desires that all of His children will be able to enjoy the blessing of eternal life, which is the promise of an eternal association with Him. This scripture concisely and specifically spells out the formula for obtaining that great gift, and each aspect of the formula requires action on our part.

Anyone who has ever been out in a strong wind knows that walking into that wind requires determined and consistent effort in order to make any progress toward our destination; it requires us to press forward in order to not be thwarted in our efforts. Therefore, the words *pressing forward* are well and wisely chosen. They do not imply a casual stroll or aimless wandering. The personal effort required and the direction of our footsteps is clearly spelled out, as is the importance of our commitment to Christ.

In order to be committed to anyone, we must know a great deal about that person—and when we speak of being committed to Christ, the surest way to know about Him is to study the scriptures, which contain the words of Christ. And once again, we note the precise selection of the word *feasting*, which implies the consumption of a bountiful, robust, and hearty meal rather than a dainty snack. It is one area in which we never need to feel guilty about overindulging.

The final part of the formula tells us we must endure to the end—despite hardships, adversity, setbacks, and disappointments. Again, the word *endure* clearly carries a call to action, an admonition to make every effort to withstand the trials and temptations that may beset us and to stand firm in our faith in the Lord Jesus Christ. James exhorts us hopefully when he says, "Take, my brethren, the prophets, who have spoken in the name of the

> The Savior desires that all of His children will be able to enjoy the blessing of eternal life, which is the promise of an eternal association with Him.

Lord, for an example of suffering in affliction, and of patience. Behold, we count them happy which endure" (James 5:10–11). The Savior Himself makes this promise to those who endure to the end in faith: "Behold, I am the law, and the light. Look unto me, and endure to the end, and ye shall live; for unto him that endureth to the end will I give eternal life" (3 Ne. 15:9), an inheritance well worth claiming.

"And, if you keep my commandments and endure to the end you shall have eternal life, which gift is the greatest of all the gifts of God" (D&C 14:7).

The Light, Life, and Truth of the World

And whatsoever thing persuadeth men to do good is of me; for good cometh of none save it be of me. I am the same that leadeth men to all good. . . . For behold, I am the Father, I am the light, and the life, and the truth of the world.

ETHER 4:12

The Savior teaches us in this scripture that He is the source of all that is good in this world and in our lives. As the Light of the world, He is the antidote to all that is dark and uncertain. In times when severe storms occasion power outages, we quickly seek alternate sources of light—candles, kerosene lamps, flashlights. However, these light sources provide only minimal and limited light in their immediate vicinity. We realize how dependent we are on electricity, and how easily that source of light can be eliminated by the forces of nature. How grateful we are when full power is restored, and all of our surroundings are fully and adequately illuminated.

The Savior is a source of light that never fails us. His Light is eternal and everlasting and provides a constant source of power that persuades and encourages us to do that which is right so that we can continuously bask in its glory without fear of a "power failure." We rejoice with the Psalmist when he proclaims, "The Lord is my light and my salvation; whom shall I fear? The Lord is the strength of my life; of whom shall I be afraid?" (Ps. 27:1).

For plants and animals alike, light is synonymous with life—and so it is with our spirits. Christ is the Light that lifts and nourishes our drooping spirits, infusing them with life and truth.

> *The Savior is a source of light that never fails us.*

Elder Dallin H. Oaks explains it beautifully. He teaches us that Jesus Christ is the source of *light* in the world and in our lives personally. The power of His example shows us the way and encourages us to do our best. He goes on to say that because of His Resurrection and Atonement, Jesus Christ gives us *life* and deliverance in both a physical and spiritual context (see "The Light and the Life," *New Era*, Dec. 1996, 4).

Jesus is the Good Shepherd whose Light and Life show us the way. Wherever He leads, we can safely follow.

> *"Lead, kindly Light, amid th'encircling gloom;*
> *Lead thou me on!*
> *The night is dark, and I am far from home; Lead thou me on!*
> *Keep thou my feet; I do not ask to see*
> *The distant scene—one step enough for me"* (Hymns, no. 97).

MISSIONARY WORK

For behold, thus said Jesus Christ, the Son of God, unto his disciples who should tarry, yea, and also to all his disciples, in the hearing of the multitude: Go ye into all the world, and preach the gospel to every creature.

MORM. 9:22

The good news of the gospel is designed to be preached to every nation, kindred, tongue, and people until it fills the whole earth. A worldwide army of missionaries—young and old, male and female—is faithfully heeding this sacred call to serve the Lord. But the call, as this scripture indicates, is to all His disciples, and that includes every member of The Church of Jesus Christ of Latter-day Saints. Whether or not we have already served or will at some future date serve in an official capacity as missionaries, we each have the responsibility to preach the gospel, for "it becometh every man who hath been warned to warn his neighbor" (D&C 88:81).

Missionary work is not a spectator sport, where we can comfortably sit on the sidelines and cheer for our favorite fellowmen. It is, as the phrase says, *work*. It is active participation and involvement in God's work and glory, extending the blessings of His gospel to our friends, our neighbors, our associates, our family members. It is living so that our example invites rather than repels others, so that we can be believed rather than despised. The old saying "What you do rings so loudly in my ears that I cannot hear what you say" has particular application to our missionary efforts. The message of the gospel will fall on deaf ears if our behavior belies our words. The Apostle Paul admonishes us to "be thou an example of the believers, in word, in conversation, in charity, in spirit, in faith, in purity" (1 Tim. 4:12). We can all be member missionaries by the power of our example. In a talk given at general conference in April 2001, Elder Jeffrey R. Holland made the observation that in order to be effective missionaries, we must first be exemplary members of The Church of Jesus Christ of Latter-day Saints (see "Witnesses Unto Me," *Ensign*, May 2001, 14).

And Elder Russell M. Nelson reminds us that as worthy disciples of Jesus Christ, we can all serve as missionaries in sharing the gospel with loved ones and all our acquaintances (see "Be Thou an Example of the Believers," *Ensign*, Nov. 2010, 49).

The Lord tells us that "the worth of souls is great in the sight of

> *We can all be member missionaries by the power of our example.*

God" (D&C 18:10). Notice that He did not say that only some souls are worthwhile, or that some are greater than others. His desire is that *all* of His children will be given the opportunity to hear and accept the full blessings of the restored gospel. We, as members of The Church of Jesus Christ of Latter-day Saints, have been graciously invited by the Savior to participate in this great work, the wages for which are richly rewarding. "And if it so be that you should labor all your days in crying repentance unto this people, and bring save it be one soul unto me, how great shall be your joy with him in the kingdom of my Father!" (D&C 18:15).

&

"Ours the sacred mission is to bear thy message far"
(Hymns, *no. 305*).

WICKEDNESS NEVER WAS HAPPINESS

Do not suppose, because it has been spoken concerning restoration, that ye shall be restored from sin to happiness. Behold, I say unto you, wickedness never was happiness.

ALMA 41:10

We live in a society where happiness is too often equated with the pleasure of self-indulgence, self-gratification, and self-absorption; with the need to be instantly rewarded and entertained, regardless of personal effort or worthiness. It is fleeting and elusive and all too often counterfeit in its end results. Contrast this, if you will, with what the scriptures teach us about the true nature of happiness. Mosiah equates happiness with obedience to the commandments of God: "I would desire that you would consider on the blessed and happy state of those who keep the commandments of God. For behold, they are blessed in all things, both temporal and spiritual; and if they hold out faithful to the end they are received into heaven, that thereby they may dwell with God in a state of never-ending happiness" (Mosiah 2:41).

The prophet Mormon mourned the tragedy of his fallen people who sorrowed "because the Lord would not always suffer them to take happiness in sin" (Morm. 2:13). It is clear that we cannot have it both ways. Darkness cannot be light, wrong cannot be right, and wickedness cannot be happiness; otherwise, the purposes of God would be frustrated. Mercy cannot rob justice. Contrast the fallen people of whom Mormon spoke with such a heavy heart with the Nephites and Lamanites, who after the resurrected Lord's ministry among them were all converted to the Church of Christ and who experienced neither "envyings, nor strifes, nor tumults, nor whoredoms, nor lyings, nor murders, nor any manner of lasciviousness; and surely there could not be a happier people among all the people who had been created by the hand of God" (4 Ne. 1:16). Quite simply stated, they were happy because they were obedient to the laws of God. And because they were obedient, they were at peace.

The words of the Psalmist reinforce this truth: "Many sorrows shall be to the wicked: but he that trusteth in the Lord, mercy shall compass him about. Be glad [happy] in the Lord, and rejoice, ye righteous: and shout for joy, all ye that are upright in heart" (Ps. 32:10–11). There is much shouting among those who are wicked, but never do they shout for joy. "There

> *We cannot have it both ways. Darkness cannot be light, wrong cannot be right, and wickedness cannot be happiness.*

is no peace, saith my God, unto the wicked" (Isa. 57:21). Proverbs 16:20 tells us that "whoso trusteth in the Lord, happy is he"; and in Proverbs 29:18 we read, "he that keepeth the law, happy is he."

The law of the harvest teaches us that we reap what we sow. If we sow the seeds of obedience, we will reap a rich harvest of peace and happiness.

❧

*"Sow a thought, and you reap an act;
Sow an act, and you reap a habit;
Sow a habit, and you reap a character;
Sow a character, and you reap a destiny."
—Ralph Waldo Emerson*

God Hears and Answers Prayers

Yea, I know that God will give liberally to him that asketh. Yea, my God will give me, if I ask not amiss; therefore I will lift up my voice unto thee; yea, I will cry unto thee, my God, the rock of my righteousness. Behold, my voice shall forever ascend up unto thee, my rock and mine everlasting God. Amen.

2 Ne. 4:35

These words bring to mind the experience of the Prophet Joseph Smith, who read the words found in James 1:5: "If any of you lack wisdom, let him ask of God, that giveth to all men liberally, and upbraideth not; and it shall be given him." Joseph Smith heeded the further words of James, "But let him ask in faith, nothing wavering" (v. 6). As he knelt to pray, putting these words to the test, Joseph's faith never wavered, even when the very jaws of hell gaped open to destroy him. Exerting all his powers of faith, he called on God to deliver him, a prayer heard and answered with the most profound results. Joseph's prayer was a prayer of faith that set the pattern for ensuing and ongoing heavenly communications as he became the instrument of Restoration, the Prophet and seer of the Lord who "has done more, save Jesus only, for the salvation of men in this world, than any other man that ever lived in it" (D&C 135:3).

Nephi's experiences with prayer were also remarkable. In answer to his prayers he saw visions, he obtained the brass plates of Laban under the most frightening and adverse circumstances, he built a ship, and he weathered the storms of life-threatening persecution from within his own family. There were no quick and easy fixes for Nephi's trials, but at no time did he give up and decide that God was not listening—**instead** he bore testimony of God's generous and liberal help and affirmed that his voice would ascend up to God forever. Because of his unwavering faith, Nephi remained firm and true in a close relationship with God through fervent and consistent prayer.

The key to effective prayer, then, is faith—faith that we will receive an answer from a God who knows us and loves us, who knows our needs and when and how those needs will best be met, "for your Father knoweth what things ye have need of before ye ask him" (Matt. 6:8). The Lord "heareth the prayer of the righteous" (Prov. 15:29).

> *The key to effective prayer, then, is faith—faith that we will receive an answer from a God who knows us and loves us, who knows our needs and when and how those needs will best be met.*

President Gordon B. Hinckley counseled us that we should expect answers to our prayers. Rather than just placing our orders with the Lord, as we would do a grocery list, we need to think carefully about what we are praying for and to whom we are speaking. Then we must listen prayerfully and respectfully for His answer (see *Teachings of Gordon B. Hinckley* [Salt Lake City: Deseret Book, 1997], 469).

❧

"And whatsoever ye shall ask the Father in my name, which is right, believing that ye shall receive, behold it shall be given unto you" (3 Ne. 18:20).

COME, LISTEN TO A PROPHET'S VOICE

My brethren, all ye that have assembled yourselves together, you that can hear my words which I shall speak to you this day; for I have not commanded you to come up hither to trifle with the words which I shall speak, but that you should hearken unto me, and open your ears that ye may hear, and your hearts that ye may understand, and your minds that the mysteries of God may be unfolded to your view.

MOSIAH 2:9

King Benjamin invited his people to a "general conference" to hear the mind and will of the Lord. His choice of words in his opening remarks is significant. He counseled his people not to trifle with his words; in other words, they were to "trifle not with sacred things" (D&C 6:12). He pleaded with them to listen with their ears *and* their hearts. This admonition recalls to our minds the words found in Proverbs 2:2 regarding how we should listen: "So that thou incline thine ear unto wisdom, and apply thine heart to understanding."

A wonderful example of this type of "listening" occurred during the Savior's ministry among the Nephites. "And their hearts were open and they did understand in their hearts the words which he prayed" (3 Ne. 19:33). If our ears, hearts, and minds are open, we are able to comprehend the mysteries of God.

Twice each year we too are invited to a general conference of the Church where we are privileged to listen to the inspired words of prophets, seers, and revelators and other General

Authorities, where "the mysteries of God may be unfolded to [our] view." The word *unfolded* implies multiple layers. We stand in awe as a beautiful quilt is unfolded and we are able to see the intricacies of workmanship and the beauty of the pattern in its complete-

> *When we listen to a prophet's voice, we are listening to the Lord.*

ness. Similarly, as we receive and understand each lovely layer of gospel principles, we are led to even greater truths as God's mysteries are revealed to us through His prophets.

When we listen to a prophet's voice, we are listening to the Lord. "What I the Lord have spoken, I have spoken, and I excuse not myself; and though the heavens and the earth pass away, my word shall not pass away, but shall all be fulfilled, whether by my own voice or by the voice of my servants, it is the same" (D&C 1:38). They are not words to be taken lightly or option-ally. Prophets are the mouthpieces of God, and through them, we are privileged to be recipients of His words.

"And they shall give heed unto these words and trifle not, and I will bless them. Amen" (D&C 32:5).

OUR PRIORITIES

But before ye seek for riches, seek ye for the kingdom of God. And after ye have obtained a hope in Christ ye shall obtain riches, if ye seek them; and ye will seek them for the intent to do good—to clothe the naked, and to feed the hungry, and to liberate the captive, and administer relief to the sick and the afflicted.

JACOB 2:18–19

When he asked the Savior what he must do to obtain eternal life, a rich young man was saddened by the Savior's answer. This otherwise good and God-fearing man could not fathom giving away his material possessions to the poor in order to truly follow Christ and enter His kingdom. He did not understand that "riches are not for ever" (Prov. 27:24).

In another time, when a young king was told by the Lord that he could ask for anything he desired, he asked for an understanding heart rather than wealth. Solomon's choice was pleasing to the Lord, who gave him great riches as well. And for a time, Solomon kept his priorities aligned with the building up of the kingdom of God. Sadly, however, he too lost his focus and God's favor.

In order to be eligible for citizenship in the kingdom of God, our hearts must be set on spiritual endeavors rather than on the accumulation of worldly wealth. This certainly does not mean that the Lord rejects those who do well in a material sense, but He is always mindful of what comes first in our lives and on what our hearts are truly set. When we are blessed materially, we are expected to be generous and compassionate in sharing our good fortune with those less fortunate. We read the words of the Savior in 3 Nephi where He says, "Give to him that asketh thee, and from him that would borrow of thee turn thou not away" (3 Ne. 12:42). He expects us to use our material treasures well and wisely while we can.

The Savior taught His disciples, "For where your treasure is, there will your heart be also. . . . No man can serve two masters; for either he will hate the one and love the other, or else he will hold to the one and despise the other. Ye cannot serve God and mammon" (3 Ne. 13:21, 24). This implies single-mindedness on our part. Elder Neal A. Maxwell explained this concept: "Even if we decide to leave Babylon, some of us endeavor to keep a second residence there, or we commute on weekends" (*Neal A. Maxwell Quote Book* [Salt Lake City: Bookcraft, 1997], 25). One foot cannot be in each camp, but must be planted firmly together on God's path.

> *In order to be eligible for citizenship in the kingdom of God, our hearts must be set on spiritual endeavors rather than on the accumulation of worldly wealth.*

When our hearts are set on obtaining a place in the kingdom of God, everything else will naturally fall into place. Spiritual and temporal blessings will work in tandem as we seek to follow and serve the one and only true Master.

❧

"Seek not for riches but for wisdom, and behold, the mysteries of God shall be unfolded unto you, and then shall you be made rich. Behold, he that hath eternal life is rich" (D&C 6:7).

DELIGHTING IN THE SCRIPTURES

For my soul delighteth in the scriptures, and my heart pondereth them. . . . Behold, my soul delighteth in the things of the Lord; and my heart pondereth continually upon the things which I have seen and heard.

2 Ne. 4:15–16

The scriptures are a rare possession that we must each discover and rediscover for ourselves. Rather than taking them for granted, we must take delight in them, as the prophet Nephi exhorts us. The words *delight* and *ponder* are words that Nephi repeats, so they must be significant. The Psalmist declares that "Thy testimonies are also my delight and my counselors" (Ps. 119:24). Clearly, as we immerse ourselves in the scriptures, we find personal joy as well as words of wisdom. When we ponder what we have read, we weigh and reflect and meditate; we absorb it into our spirits; we liken it to our lives as recommended by Nephi: "for I did liken all scriptures unto us, that it might be for our profit and learning" (1 Ne. 19:23).

It is better to read carefully, to ponder a small section of sacred writ, rather than to quickly skim mere words in order to meet a scripture-reading goal. We should constantly ask ourselves the questions, "What does this mean *to* me?" "What does this mean *for* me?" "How can I integrate this scripture into my life?"

The Savior gives us the perfect reason for studying the scriptures: "Search the scriptures; for in them ye think ye have eternal life: and they are they which testify of me" (John 5:39). The scriptures are where we learn of Him and become acquainted with His voice. "And whoso receiveth not my voice is not acquainted with my voice, and is not of me" (D&C 84:52). The scriptures are the Lord's love letters to us. President Gordon B. Hinckley explained that for him, reading the scriptures was a labor of love rather than a task oriented toward scriptural scholarship (see "Feasting upon the Scriptures," *Ensign*, Dec. 1985).

The scriptures enrich our minds and expand our spirits. We learn great and powerful lessons as we read and delight in and ponder holy words dictated by our Heavenly Father and His Son Jesus Christ. What lessons do we learn from the scriptures? We learn of ethical standards, proper spiritual living, the rewards of righteousness and the wages of sin, the nature of the Godhead, the formula for repentance and the miracle of forgiveness, the joy of service, and the importance of mission-

> *The scriptures are the Lord's love letters to us.*

ary work, to name just a few. But most importantly we learn about the great gift of the Atonement and the reality of the Resurrection.

President Joseph Fielding Smith teaches us that we should *treasure* the Lord's words. This means not only reading and studying, but humbly and obediently seeking to do the Lord's will, thus inviting His wisdom and inspiration as we read (see *Doctrines of Salvation* [Salt Lake City: Bookcraft, 1954], Vol. 1, 305).

Regarding the joy we will receive when we study holy writ, the Prophet Joseph Smith made this insightful observation: "He who reads it oftenest will like it best" (*Teachings of the Prophet Joseph Smith* [Salt Lake City: Deseret Book, 1976], 56).

> *"And whoso treasureth up my word, shall not be deceived"* (JS—M 1:37).

Qualities of Disciples of Christ

And now I would that ye should be humble, and be submissive and gentle; easy to be entreated; full of patience and long-suffering; being temperate in all things; being diligent in keeping the commandments of God at all times; asking for whatsoever things ye stand in need, both spiritual and temporal; always returning thanks unto God for whatsoever things ye do receive.

Alma 7:23

In this scripture, Alma entreats us to be humble, submissive, patient, diligent, prayerful, and grateful, qualities that all disciples of Jesus Christ should possess. It is our privilege and responsibility to become Christ's disciples or followers, and it is through the gospel that we learn how to faithfully follow Him. The gospel is the way of discipleship; in other words, we are all pupils with a Divine Tutor. Christ's example perfectly fulfills all the requirements that Alma lists for true discipleship.

Alma's list may seem a bit daunting, but it is well for us to remember that discipleship is a process, not an event; it is a lifelong race of endurance. It is, in a way, our spiritual Olympics. We all qualify for the race. There is no comparison by title, position, or station in life. There is only one criteria: Do we have enough faith in and love for our Savior Jesus Christ to do the will of God? We live in a society of "instant" products and gratifications, but it is wise for us to remember that discipleship is not whipped up in an instant, like a pudding.

Alma speaks of patience and long-suffering. Disciples have staying power—not just during the easy times, but in times of adversity as well. We cannot always choose the obstacles we face, but we can always decide whether we will allow them to discourage us and pull us down, or lead us to a closer dependence on our Savior. The Savior encourages us to hang on with patience, even when we cannot see any purpose behind our misery. He tells us, "If thou wilt do good, yea, and hold out faithful to the end, thou shalt be saved in the kingdom of God" (D&C 6:13).

Love is truly another symbol of one's discipleship. We become followers of His divine example by

> *The gospel is the way of discipleship; in other words, we are pupils with a Divine Tutor.*

reaching out in acts of kindness, forgiveness, grace, and the love of which the Savior speaks—a message so important that it was one of His last admonitions to His beloved Apostles—"love one another" (John 14:34).

President Dieter F. Uchtdorf reminds us that discipleship is a refining and purifying process. It is an inviting pilgrimage of personal progress that we can each begin here and now, without any prerequisites. It is our privilege to embrace the gospel and become His disciples (see "The Way of the Disciple," *Ensign*, May 2009, 76–77).

Discipleship requires action. We must learn to be doers of the word and not hearers only (see James 1:22).

The Power of Unwavering Faith

Wherefore, we search the prophets, and we have many revelations and the spirit of prophecy; and having all these witnesses we obtain a hope, and our faith becometh unshaken, insomuch that we truly can command in the name of Jesus and the very trees obey us, or the mountains, or the waves of the sea.

JACOB 4:6

Faith is a powerful principle with a powerful promise. "If ye have faith as a grain of mustard seed, ye shall say to the mountain, Remove hence to yonder place; and it shall remove; and nothing shall be impossible unto you" (Matt. 17:20).

It was faith that allowed the brother of Jared to seek and then see the Lord. It was faith that allowed the lepers to be healed, the blind to see, and the woman with the issue of blood to be made whole. "Daughter, be of good comfort: thy faith hath made thee whole; go in peace" (Luke 8:48).

Faith can produce physical miracles, such as the moving of mountains, the calming of a storm, the healing of physical infirmities. But the fruits of our faith are often more quiet and less spectacular. The Lord's highest priority for us is the miracle of our broken hearts—our sure and abiding faith in Him and in the healing power of His Atonement. We must focus our faith not in *our* good intentions and desires, but in the Savior's intentions for us. He sees a broader picture; He knows what we do not know; He knows our needs way better than we do. It involves a shift from what we know in our head to what we feel in our heart.

Faith moves us past fear and prompts us to focus on our Savior's love. "Fear thou not; for I am with thee: be not dismayed; for I am thy God: I will strengthen thee; yea, I will help thee; yea, I will uphold thee with the right hand of my righteousness" (Isa. 41:10).

As President Gordon B. Hinckley pronounced his benediction at the close of one of his talks, he humbly prayed for members of The Church of Jesus Christ of Latter-day Saints to have the kind of faith in the Lord that will be our guide both day and night (see "The Faith to Move Mountains," *Ensign*, Nov. 2006). What a beautiful allusion to the children of Israel as the Lord led them through their physical

> *Faith is a powerful principle with a powerful promise.*

wilderness and through the wilderness of their flagging faith—a cloud by day and a pillar by night. He extends this same promise to each of us. Faith in the Lord Jesus Christ is the hopeful and healing principle of power that will bring us safely through our "wildernesses" and past our personal storms to the promise of eternal life.

◈

In his poem "Ode to the West Wind," Percy Bysshe Shelley wrote, "O, Wind, If Winter comes, can Spring be far behind?" (Romantic and Victorian Poetry, ed. William Frost [New York: Prentice-Hall, Inc., 1950], 206). Just as we know that the green things of spring follow the dark dormancy of winter, so our faith in the Lord Jesus Christ guides us through our dark places toward Light and Life.

WALKING IN STRAIGHT PATHS

For I perceive that ye are in the paths of righteousness; I perceive that ye are in the path which leads to the kingdom of God; yea, I perceive that ye are making his paths straight. I perceive that it has been made known unto you, by the testimony of his word, that he cannot walk in crooked paths; neither doth he vary from that which he hath said; neither hath he a shadow of turning from the right to the left, or from that which is right to that which is wrong; therefore, his course is one eternal round.

ALMA 7:19–20

We are all familiar with the plight of the children of Israel who wandered for forty years in the wilderness. The pathway to the promised land was not that circuitous, yet their journey was long and arduous because they frequently forgot to walk in paths of righteousness. The Lord had made great promises to them, but they could not claim those promises until they were willing to walk the straight and narrow way. We might say that their spiritual GPS was malfunctioning.

This has been the case in all dispensations—children of God have frequently taken wrong turns, taking dangerous detours that lead away from rather than toward the kingdom of God. In all such instances, the Lord has always held out a beckoning hand with which to give true direction and encouragement that would put His children back on the right path. He will not follow after us in our crooked paths, but waits with love and patience for us to tune in to the correct spiritual frequencies that guide us safely and surely back to His loving arms. His paths are eternal and unchanging—neither the route nor the rules will ever change.

Isaiah reminds us, "his hand is stretched out still" (Isa. 9:12, 17, 21). Do we trust Him enough to reach out and take His hand? We are told that the Lord will direct our paths (see Prov. 3:5–6). Therein is the promise of a divine and unfailing spiritual GPS.

Do we believe and live the first principles and ordinances of the gospel, with the faith and fortitude to endure to the end, no matter what? Are we engaged in a daily dialogue of sincere and humble prayer? Do we love one another and show that love in word and deed? The Lord makes very clear what He expects of us: "Verily I say, men should be anxiously engaged in a good cause, and do many things of their own free will, and bring to pass much righteousness" (D&C 58:27).

> *As we follow the pathway to His kingdom, neither the route nor the rules will ever change.*

Elder Marcus B. Nash teaches that as we strive to live in obedience to God's commandments, His love will quench our thirsting spirits and renew our desire to reach upward toward Him (see "Cultivating Righteousness," *Ensign*, Aug. 2008).

❧

We are reminded of Jeremiah's prophetic promise to those who walk in straight paths: "For he shall be as a tree planted by the waters, and that spreadeth out her roots by the river, and shall not see when heat cometh, but her leaf shall be green; and shall not be careful in the year of drought, neither shall cease from yielding fruit" (Jer. 17:8).

37 HOPE

And what is it that ye shall hope for? Behold I say unto you that ye shall have hope through the atonement of Christ and the power of his resurrection, to be raised up to life eternal, and this because of your faith in him according to the promise. Wherefore, if a man have faith he must needs have hope; for without faith there cannot be any hope.

MORO. 7:41–42

The virtues of faith, hope, and charity are often linked together in the scriptures. Peter taught that Christ's Atonement and Resurrection enable us to put our faith and hope in God (1 Pet. 1:21). Alma admonishes us to "have faith, hope, and charity, and then [we] will always abound in good works" (Alma 7:24). The Apostle Paul links these virtues together when he says, "And now abideth faith, hope, and charity, these three" (1 Cor. 13:13), and Moroni records the words of his father, Mormon, regarding the great virtues of faith, hope, and charity (see Moro. 7:41–47).

President Dieter F. Uchtdorf teaches us that hope is the undergirding virtue upon which faith and charity depend. Our faith may be momentarily weakened by sin or the vicissitudes of life; our charity may be challenged by our shortcomings; but our hope will strengthen and purify our efforts to cultivate these virtues (see "The Infinite Power of Hope," *Ensign*, Nov. 2008).

Moroni reminds us what it is we are to hope for and have faith in. Through Christ's Resurrection, we have the hope for an unconditional promise of immortality, an inseparable connection of our body and spirit; through His Atonement, we have the hope for eternal life, or life in the presence of our Heavenly Father and Savior. "Gospel hope is," as Elder Neal A. Maxwell tells us, "a very focused and particularized hope that is based upon jus-tified expecta-

> *What a miraculous blessing is the Atone-ment of Jesus Christ!*

tions" (*Notwithstanding My Weakness* [Salt Lake City: Deseret Book, 1981], 41). Our ultimate expectation is exaltation, made possible only through the Atonement.

What a miraculous blessing is the Atonement of Jesus Christ! It is indeed the source of hope in the gospel. It is the perfect brightness of hope spoken of by Nephi that leads to eternal life (see 2 Ne. 31:20). It is the hope and desire of the Psalmist: "For in thee, O Lord, do I hope" (Ps. 38:15). The Atonement is the very foundation upon which we build our hope and our faith.

∽≈

"The hope of the righteous shall be gladness" (Prov. 10:28).

THAT WE MIGHT HAVE JOY

Adam fell that men might be; and men are, that they might have joy.

2 Ne. 2:25

Sometimes, when the burdens of life seem a bit overwhelming, when sorrows and disappointments seem to press in from all sides, when hard work is the order of the day, we tend to forget that, as the Prophet Joseph Smith taught, "Happiness (joy) is the object and design of our existence" (*Teachings of the Prophet Joseph Smith* [Salt Lake City: Deseret Book, 1976], 255).

Consider the trials and tribulations that Adam and Eve experienced after leaving the Garden of Eden. Theirs was not an easy journey or lot in life, yet Adam spoke this marvelous and positive affirmation: "Because of my transgression my eyes are opened, and in this life I shall have joy" (Moses 5:10). That same section of scripture goes on to tell us that Adam's testimony of joy made Eve glad also, and together they "blessed the name of God" (v. 12). Let us consider briefly other scriptural examples of joy.

Shepherds on a hillside were given "good tidings of great joy" (Luke 2:10), which tidings have brought great joy into the hearts of mankind through all the intervening years. The Savior speaks generously to us of sharing His joy when He says, "These things have I spoken unto you, that my joy might remain in you, and that your joy may be full" (John 15:11).

In recounting his vision of the tree of life, Lehi speaks of partaking of the fruit of the tree, a representation of the love of God, which fruit "filled [his] soul with exceedingly great joy" (1 Ne. 8:12), and which he was anxious to share with his family. Alma speaks of the great joy we can all share "because of the resurrection of the dead, according to the will and power of deliverance of Jesus Christ from the bands of death" (Alma 4:14). Isaiah speaks directly to those of us living in the last days when he says, "For ye shall go out with joy, and be led forth with peace" (Isa. 55:12).

The Savior speaks of the joy we can experience as we share the gospel with others: "And now, if your joy shall be great with one soul that you have brought unto me into the kingdom of my Father, how great will be your joy if you should bring many souls unto me!" (D&C 18:16). John tells us that we can "have no greater joy than to hear that [our] children walk in truth" (3 Jn. 1:4). With sweet and tender compassion, the Psalmist

> *Adam spoke this marvelous and positive affirmation: "Because of my transgression my eyes are opened, and in this life I shall have joy" (Moses 5:10).*

comforts all those who have experienced sorrow and loss: "Weeping may endure for a night, but joy cometh in the morning" (Ps. 30:5). Finally, we read the moving yet powerful words of the Savior when He says, "Blessed are ye because of your faith. And now behold, my joy is full" (3 Ne. 17:20).

How can we resist the invitation to be a joyful people when our very Exemplar feels such joy? The key to finding joy in our lives is to "pursue the path that leads to it; and this path is . . . keeping all the commandments of God" (*Teachings of the Prophet Joseph Smith*, 255–256).

"And my soul shall be joyful in the Lord: it shall rejoice in his salvation" (Ps. 35:9).

Come unto Christ

Yea, come unto Christ, and be perfected in him, and deny yourselves of all ungodliness; and if ye shall deny yourselves of all ungodliness, and love God with all your might, mind, and strength, then is his grace sufficient for you, that by his grace ye may be perfect in Christ; and if by the grace of God ye are perfect in Christ, ye can in nowise deny the power of God.

Moro. 10:32

The invitation to come unto Christ is extended by the Savior Himself: "Behold, he sendeth an invitation unto all men, for the arms of mercy are extended towards them, and he saith: Repent, and I will receive you. Yea, he saith: Come unto me and ye shall partake of the fruit of the tree of life; yea, and ye shall eat and drink of the bread and the waters of life freely" (Alma 5:33–34). This imagery is familiar to us as we recall the Savior's declarations in the New Testament that He is the bread and the water of life—even eternal life, and this imagery is repeated in Revelation 22:17: "And the Spirit and the bride say, Come. And let him that heareth say, Come. And let him that is athirst come. And whosoever will, let him take the water of life freely."

He stands with open arms, ready to receive as the recipients of His grace all who will repent. Elder Tad R. Callister writes that the Savior's invitation is all-inclusive, and it is not a one-time offer. The Savior waits with open arms to encircle all of His children for all of our lives. "Behold, mine arm of mercy is extended towards you, and whosoever will come, him will I receive" (3 Ne. 9:14) (see *The Infinite Atonement* [Salt Lake City: Deseret Book, 2000], 28).

The Savior's role as our Redeemer is clear. "Wherefore, all mankind were in a lost and in a fallen state, and ever would be save they should rely on this Redeemer" (1 Ne. 10:6). There are no efforts or acts we can perform that will guarantee us the perfection promised by Christ. His Atonement is infinite and all-inclusive. Our acts of repentance simply express our gratitude for and acceptance of this wondrous gift.

Regarding the Lord's invitation to come unto Him, Elder Jeffrey R. Holland assures us that God's divine embrace is available to all who seek it.

> *The invitation to come unto Christ is extended by the Savior Himself.*

No matter what adversities we may experience, His Atonement guarantees us safety and peace (see *Trusting Jesus* [Salt Lake City: Deseret Book, 2001], 66).

In denying ourselves of all ungodliness, we make the commitment to "love and serve him, the only living and true God" (D&C 20:19). We signify that we are willing to "stand as witnesses of God at all times and in all things, and in all places that [we] may be in even until death" (Mosiah 18:9) in order to be candidates for the first resurrection and eternal life. We willingly take upon ourselves "the name of Christ, having a determination to serve him to the end" (Moro. 6:3).

"Behold, mine arm of mercy is extended towards you, and whosoever will come, him will I receive" (3 Ne. 9:14).

EARNEST PRAYER

And my soul hungered; and I kneeled down before my Maker, and I cried unto him in mighty prayer and supplication for mine own soul; and all the day long did I cry unto him; yea, and when the night came I did still raise my voice high that it reached the heavens. And there came a voice unto me, saying: Enos, thy sins are forgiven thee, and thou shalt be blessed. . . . because of thy faith in Christ, whom thou has never before heard nor seen. . . . Wherefore, go to, thy faith hath made thee whole.

ENOS 1:4–5, 8

We have all experienced the pangs of physical hunger, and know how it feels to have that need satisfied by a good and nourishing meal. During our moments of acute hunger, our minds often dwell longingly on our favorite foods, and we happily anticipate the moment when our every culinary desire will be gratified.

Do we experience that same degree of spiritual hunger? Do we think of the times when we have taken our fears and pains and doubts and problems to the Lord and then experienced the healing and comforting balm of His helping hand, and do we long for that spiritual appeasement yet again? The Savior tells us that it is good for our souls to hunger: "Blessed are they who do hunger and thirst after righteousness, for they shall be filled with the Holy Ghost" (3 Ne. 12:6). This is surely the ultimate spiritual sustenance.

The words of Enos invite us to seek nourishment for our souls through the avenue of regular, heartfelt, and earnest prayer—prayer that is humbly offered as we kneel before our Maker (the very act of getting on our knees shows our respect and reverence for Deity); prayer that is neither rote nor rushed (not an exercise that is part of a checklist); prayer that is constant and consistent (not just when we are in trouble); prayer that is motivated by our faith in the Lord Jesus Christ (we truly believe that He lives and loves us); prayer that reaches the heavens and then waits respectfully for the Lord's response (we understand that sometimes we must wait on the Lord, who knows best how and when to respond to our petitions).

We have the Lord's personal assurance that He hears and answers our prayers. "And ye shall seek me, and find me, when ye shall search for me with all your heart" (Jer. 29:13). "Be thou humble; and the Lord thy God shall lead thee by the hand, and give thee answer to thy prayers" (D&C 112:10).

> *"Blessed are they who do hunger and thirst after righteousness, for they shall be filled with the Holy Ghost" (3 Ne. 12:6).*

Prayer not only refreshes and feeds our souls, but refines them as well. The Lord's promise that our hunger and thirst for righteousness will be assuaged by the companionship of the Holy Ghost is a promise that applies to our personal prayers. As we humbly, earnestly, and consistently pray in faith, we experience the Lord's cleansing power and the comforting companionship of the Holy Ghost.

"Whatsoever ye ask the Father in my name it shall be given unto you, that is expedient for you" (D&C 88:64).

The Savior's Birth

Lift up your head and be of good cheer; for behold the time is at hand, and on this night shall the sign be given, and on the morrow come I into the world, to show unto the world that I will fulfill all that which I have caused to be spoken by the mouth of my holy prophets.

3 Ne. 1:13

This is surely one of the most lovely and poignant scriptures in the Book of Mormon. After waiting and watching for the fulfillment of the prophecy spoken by Samuel the Lamanite regarding the birth of the Savior, the faithful Nephites, hounded and hunted and humiliated by the unbelievers, faced sure and certain death at their hands "on the morrow." As a prophet of God bowed himself in humble prayer, the voice of the Savior Himself brought the sweet assurance that the dawning of the next morning would be Christmas morning.

The phrase *lift up your head* is an invitation to all of us to look heavenward and give reverent thanks for and appropriate observance of this great advent. Like Mary, it is well for us to keep "all these things, and ponder . . . them in [our] heart[s]" (see Luke 2:19).

The traditions of Christmas celebrate "good tidings of great joy." As we lift up our heads in honor of these good tidings, do our Christmas traditions make Christ the central focus—do we make sure that the lights, the decorations, the gifts, the feasting, and the beloved stories all serve as reminders of the gift of the Son of God? Do we make sure that the glitter does not overshadow God's glorious gift to us, that receiving does not become more important than giving, that our celebrations magnify rather than minimize the coming of the Lord?

Christmas is a time of opportunity to gather our families around us and instill in them traditions of sacred truths. It is a time to adorn our homes in ways that make the Savior the centerpiece of our celebrations. It is a time to search the scriptures and ponder, as did Mary, on the miracle of His birth and life. It is a time to make a joyful noise unto the Lord as we lift our voices in the traditional and beautiful Christmas carols.

It is a time to review with our families the sacred and breathtaking words of Isaiah: "For unto us a child is born, unto us a son is given: and the government shall be upon his shoulder: and his name shall be called Wonderful, Counsellor, The mighty God, The everlasting Father, The Prince of Peace" (Isa. 9:6).

> *The phrase "lift up your head" is an invitation to all of us to look heavenward and give reverent thanks for and appropriate observance of this great advent.*

Christmas is a time to remember with joy the signs given on the American continent as the believers awaited this glorious event. It is a time to remind our children of the Savior's magnificent words of comfort and peace as He said to Helaman's grandson, the prophet Nephi, "Lift up your head and be of good cheer; for behold, the time is at hand" (3 Ne. 1:13).

"For unto you is born this day in the city of David a Saviour, which is Christ the Lord" (Luke 2:11).

DAUGHTERS OF GOD

Put on thy beautiful garments, O daughter of Zion.

MORO. 10:31

Our strength as daughters of Zion—as daughters of God—is measured by the strength of our faith in the Lord Jesus Christ and our trust in His redeeming love and infinite Atonement. His is a pure love that "never faileth. . . . and it endureth forever; and whoso is found possessed of it at the last day, it shall be well with [her]" (Moro. 7:46–47).

This glorious promise enlarges our vision, enables us to enjoy the blessings and beauties of this world, and encourages us to "look to God and live" (Alma 37:47). Guided by this eternal perspective, our potential is truly wondrous—a magnificent canvas upon which to create a masterpiece worthy of God's acceptance.

"Who can find a virtuous woman? for her price is far above rubies" (Prov. 31:10).

Regardless of the season of life in which we presently find ourselves, these words are encouraging, uplifting, and pertinent. We can and should be engaged in the virtue of good works, serving others selflessly, stretching out our hand to the poor and needy, clothing ourselves with strength and honor, speaking words of kindness and wisdom, inspiring trust and confidence in others.

One of the ways in which we as women can increase our faith in the Lord Jesus Christ and thus claim the blessings of the Atonement is by being anxiously engaged in good works. We relate to the metaphor of this proverb: "She . . . worketh willingly with her hands. . . . She looketh well to the ways of her household, and eateth not the bread of idleness" (Prov. 31:13, 27). The word *work* appears countless times throughout the scriptures and is an ethic lauded and rewarded by the Lord. "Well done, thou good and faithful servant" (Matt. 25:21). It is a word well-known to women, who take pride in their labors and satisfaction in a job well done. What greater compliment can we hope to receive from our Heavenly Father than

> *Our strength as daughters of God is measured by our faith in the Lord Jesus Christ and His redeeming love.*

to have Him say to us, "Many daughters have done virtuously, but thou excellest them all" (Prov. 31:29).

President Gordon B. Hinckley reiterates Moroni's gracious exhortation as he encourages women to live up to our divine potential. As daughters of God, we are assured of His love and approval. He has entrusted us with a noble work that we alone can do. It is our privilege to walk in confidence, knowing that we are an integral part of God's kingdom, trusted workers in His vineyard (see "Live up to Your Inheritance," *Ensign*, Nov. 1983, 83–84).

⚜

"But a woman that feareth the Lord, she shall be praised"
(Prov. 31:30).

OPPOSITION IN ALL THINGS

For it must needs be that there is an opposition in all things. If not so . . . righteousness could not be brought to pass, neither wickedness, neither holiness nor misery, neither good nor bad.

2 NE. 2:11

None of us passes through this earthly experience unscathed or untouched by adversity in one form or another, whether it be pain or heartache or disappointment or some other form of misfortune. President Gordon B. Hinckley once said that all too often we think that our lives should be untroubled by adversity; but he went on to say that "even adversity has some sweet uses" (see "God Shall Give unto You Knowledge by His Holy Spirit," *BYU Speeches of the Year*, Sept. 25, 1973, 105–106).

What are these sweet uses? We cannot always choose the obstacles we face, but we can always decide whether we will allow them to discourage us or lead us to a closer relationship with and dependence on our Savior. When we feel that our endurance has been tested and stretched to the breaking point, it is well for us to remember that "the Lord is [our] shepherd" who will help us find green pastures that refresh us after traversing the barren wastelands of our afflictions; He will lead us to still waters that calm us after enduring the winds and the waves of personal storms; He will comfort and strengthen us after we have experienced death's sorrowful sting; He will nourish us with the good and pleasing word of God that allows us to lift up our head in faith when confronted by enemies; He will bless us with His unfailing and eternal goodness and mercy (see Ps. 23).

Elder Neal A. Maxwell reminded us that God knows what our limits are, and He will not allow us to be tested beyond what we can endure. However, He also knows that the fires of affliction serve not only to test us but to refine and perfect us (see *All These Things Shall Give Thee Experience* [Salt Lake City: Deseret Book, 1979], 46).

The Prophet Joseph Smith knew well the furnace of affliction and "opposition in all things." On occasions too numerous to mention, he experienced trials and hardships that took him very nearly to the edge of human endurance. In the degrading circumstances of Liberty Jail, he cried out to the Lord. And then came the Lord's splendid and reassuring response: "My son, peace be unto thy soul; thine adversity and thine afflictions shall be but a small moment; And then, if thou endure it well, God shall exalt thee on high; thou shalt triumph over all thy foes. . . . know thou, my son, that all these things

> *We cannot always choose the obstacles we face, but we can always decide whether we will allow them to discourage and pull us down, or lead us to a closer relationship with and dependence on our Savior.*

shall give thee experience, and shall be for thy good" (D&C 121:7–8; 122:7).

Again and again, the Lord provided that supply of strength of which Joseph spoke and bore witness. And that strength is not something reserved only for prophets of God. He gives all of us strength to weather the winds of adversity. It is a promise and gift reserved for each one of us because we are His children; He knows us, and He loves us.

❧

"If thou wilt do good, yea, and hold out faithful to the end, thou shalt be saved in the kingdom of God" (D&C 6:13).

THE SON OF GOD

Behold, I am Jesus Christ the Son of God. I created the heavens and the earth, and all things that in them are. I was with the Father from the beginning. I am in the Father, and the Father in me; and in me hath the Father glorified his name.

3 NE. 9:15

In this declaration of His identity, the Savior reminds us that He is the literal Son of God. He is, in fact, God's only Begotten Son in the flesh. The Father Himself bore witness of this fact when He introduced the Savior to the remaining Nephite population after the great destruction that accompanied His Crucifixion: "Behold my Beloved Son, in whom I am well pleased, in whom I have glorified my name—hear ye him" (3 Ne. 11:7). Then in the dispensation of the fulness of times, the Father again made this relationship abundantly clear when both He and His Son appeared to Joseph Smith in the Sacred Grove: "This is my Beloved Son. Hear Him!" (JS—H 1:17).

Others have testified of this truth. On a certain day as Jesus talked with His Apostles, He asked this crucial question: "Whom say ye that I am?" Simon Peter answered and said, "Thou art the Christ, the Son of the living God" (Matt. 16:15–16). This was and is a precious and powerful testimony—one forged in Peter's soul as he walked and talked with the Savior. His was a testimony gained through personal revelation—a testimony strengthened by the Savior's personal ministrations.

The scriptures are replete with similar testimonies borne by prophets of old. Prophets and Apostles of this latter-day dispensation bear strong personal testimony of Him as the Son of God as well.

Can any of us ever forget the final testimony of Elder Bruce R. McConkie, an Apostle of God, who bore a humble yet powerful testimony of Christ's divine Sonship and of the reality of His role as our Savior and Redeemer? He boldly stated, "I am one of His witnesses, and in a coming day I shall feel the nail marks in his hands and in his feet and shall wet his feet with my tears. But I shall not know any better then than I know now that He is God's Almighty Son, that He is our Savior and Redeemer" ("The Purifying Power of Gethsemane," *Ensign*, May 1985, 11).

> *In this declaration of His identity, the Savior reminds us that He is the literal Son of God.*

Our own beloved prophet, Thomas S. Monson, also bears his witness of the Savior's divine Sonship, of His great atoning sacrifice, and of His glorious Resurrection (see "He Is Not Here, but Is Risen," *Ensign*, Apr. 2011, 5).

The most important thing that any of us as members of The Church of Jesus Christ of Latter-day Saints can do is to know the Savior, to know that He is indeed the Son of God, and that it is to Him that we can "look and have the gift of eternal life."

❧

"I will declare the decree: the Lord hath said unto me, Thou art my Son; this day have I begotten thee" (Ps. 2:7).

CHRIST IS THE CREATOR

And now, my sons, I speak unto you these things for your profit and learning; for there is a God, and he hath created all things, both the heavens and the earth, and all things that in them are, both things to act and things to be acted upon.

2 NE. 2:14

As we take time to look around us, we cannot help but be filled with a sense of wonder as we behold the beauties of the earth. Regardless of where we live, we see the grandeur of nature—whether it be rolling prairies, majestic mountains, vast oceans, small lakes and streams, abundant forests, deserts with their ever-changing sands, or lush and green locales.

All these wonders bear witness of the Creator, and prophets of all dispensations bear witness that Jesus Christ is that Creator. Moses records the Savior's words: "And worlds without number have I created" (Moses 1:33). King Benjamin witnesses: "For we believe in Jesus Christ, the Son of God, who created heaven and earth, and all things" (Mosiah 4:2). John, the beloved Apostle, testifies, "All things were made by him; and without him was not anything made that was made" (John 1:3). Isaiah records the Lord's affirmation of His creative wonders: "I will plant in the wilderness the cedar, the shittah tree, and the myrtle, and the oil tree; I will set in the desert the fir tree, and the pine, and the box tree together: That they may see, and know, and consider, and understand together, that the hand of the Lord hath done this, and the Holy One of Israel hath created it" (Isa. 41:19–20). And to the Prophet Joseph Smith, the

Lord declared, "Behold, I am Jesus Christ, the Son of the Living God, who created the heavens and the earth" (D&C 14:9).

Elder Mark E. Petersen explains that the creation of the earth was planned and purposeful. God the Father was the Architect, and Jesus Christ was the Creator (see "Creator and Savior," *Ensign*, May, 1983).

Ralph Waldo Emerson wrote that nature or creation is the symbol of God's reality (see *The Essays of Ralph Waldo Emerson* [Cambridge, Massachusetts: Hanover University Press, 1987], 317–322). Nature captures the essence of the splendor of both creations and the Creator, whether we are looking upward into the wonders of the firmament, or beholding the breathtaking

> *All these wonders bear witness of the Creator, and prophets of all dispensations bear witness that Jesus Christ is that Creator.*

beauty of earthly landscapes that range from majestic mountains, to splendid forests, to mighty oceans or gentle streams, or to luxuriant rolling prairies.

King Benjamin bears testimony of Christ as the Creator, and invites each of us to do the same: "Believe in God; believe that he is, and that he created all things, both in heaven and in earth; believe that he has all wisdom, and all power, both in heaven and in earth" (Mosiah 4:9).

∽✦

"Behold, the Lord hath created the earth . . . and he hath created his children that they should possess it" (1 Ne. 17:36).

The Savior's Mercy and Love

O ye house of Israel whom I have spared, how oft will I gather you as a hen gathereth her chickens under her wings, if ye will repent and return unto me with full purpose of heart.

3 Ne. 10:6

The Lord is ever mindful of us and of our need to repent. Notice that in this scripture, He tells us He *will* gather us, not that He *would have*, but now it is too late. His call to repentance is all-inclusive and ongoing; there is no exclusionary clause and no expiration date.

The Savior's metaphor of a mother hen with her baby chicks is particularly tender and vivid. Anyone who has witnessed such a "gathering" knows that those little chicks are grateful for the large and willing wings that protect and warm and love them. They scurry obediently from their scattered locations as their mother bids them to come. We are offered that same invitation to feel the tender embrace of the Savior's warm and welcoming and protective arms. "Behold, mine arm of mercy is extended towards you, and whosoever will come, him will I receive; and blessed are those who come unto me" (3 Ne. 9:14).

During the Savior's earthly ministry, many people with physical infirmities and afflictions flocked to Him to be recipients of His healing powers. Likewise, He desires to heal our spiritual infirmities, but He can accomplish this only if we are willing to repent and change our actions and the intent of our hearts—to leave our disparate wanderings from the straight and narrow and run toward His "healing wings." His words are clear and encouraging: "Blessed are they who will repent and turn unto me" (Hel. 13:11); "Return unto me and I will return unto you, saith the Lord of Hosts" (3 Ne. 24:7). Clearly, the Lord expects us to correct our course according to our individual circumstances. Sometimes we create our own detours and shortcuts that take us into the unsafe territories of pride or anger, or other forms of sin. Yet the Lord always gives us the opportunity to adjust our direction of travel, to turn around and embrace His ways and His laws.

The Lord speaks of His promise to those who will repent, change their course, and hasten to be gathered in His loving arms. "Then will I sprinkle clean water upon you, and ye shall be clean. . . . A new heart also will I give you, and a new spirit will I put within you: and I will take away the stony heart out of your flesh, and I will give you an heart of flesh" (Ezek. 36:25–26). These words remind us that our new heart will be a broken heart, and our new spirit will be a contrite spirit: "And whoso cometh unto me with a broken heart and a contrite spirit, him will I baptize with fire and with the Holy Ghost" (3 Ne. 9:20).

> *His call to repentance is all-inclusive and ongoing; there is no exclusionary clause and no expiration date.*

"O hope of ev'ry contrite heart, O joy of all the meek,

To those who fall, how kind thou art! How good to those who seek" (*Hymns*, no. 141).

※

"Yea, in the shadow of thy wings will I make my refuge"
(Ps. 57:1).

THE VOICE OF GOD

And it came to pass that while they were thus conversing one with another, they heard a voice as if it came out of heaven; and they cast their eyes round about, for they understood not the voice which they heard; and it was not a harsh voice, neither was it a loud voice; nevertheless, and notwithstanding it being a small voice it did pierce them that did hear to the center, insomuch that there was no part of their frame that it did not cause to quake; yea, it did pierce them to the very soul, and did cause their hearts to burn.

3 NE. 11:3

We are surrounded by voices that compete for our attention—voices that would have us buy this or buy that, voices that would entice us to engage in one type of activity or another, voices that offer us advice that ranges from that which is sound and pleasing to that which is deceitful and debasing. The noise can often be deafening and the messages confusing.

The one voice upon which we can rely to always lead us in paths of righteousness is that of our Heavenly Father, whether it is His own voice or that of His Beloved Son. When God speaks, He does so with a voice that pierces our souls—not because it is loud and strident, but rather because it is still and small. It is a voice that speaks to our hearts and to our spirits with a message we can trust. It is "a still voice of perfect mildness, as if it had been a whisper, and it did pierce even to the very soul" (Hel. 5:30).

Just as sheep know and trust the voice of their shepherd, come when he calls, and follow wherever he leads, the Savior has told us that He is our Shepherd—a Good Shepherd whom we can trust. He knows us by name, and we must learn to listen for His voice. Like the Nephites of old or the young boy Samuel, we may need to hear His voice several times before we recognize its source and its message. However, we learn from these examples that God does not cease speaking if we don't understand immediately. It is not like a missed telephone call where we learn that if we had answered the phone, we might have won a grand prize. God is patient and persistent, and the "prize" is well within our reach.

Adam and Eve listened to the voice of God as they walked in the Garden of Eden; a youthful Joseph Smith heard the voice of God in a quiet place that was subsequently to be designated

> *The one voice upon which we can rely to always guide us in paths of righteousness is that of our Heavenly Father, whether it is His own voice or that of His Beloved Son.*

as sacred; the surviving Nephites, in a land decimated by the fury of nature's destructive forces, heard the voice of God as He introduced His Beloved Son: "Behold my Beloved Son, in whom I am well pleased, in whom I have glorified my name—hear ye him" (3 Ne. 11:7). And we too can hear His voice as we tune our hearts and spirits to hear His pleasing word through the voice of His living prophets and through the privilege of quiet and personal revelation.

❧

"And the Lord shall cause his glorious voice to be heard"
(Isa. 30:30).

The Lord's Promise to the Faithful

Therefore, repent all ye ends of the earth, and come unto me, and believe in my gospel, and be baptized in my name; for he that believeth and is baptized shall be saved. . . . And blessed is he that is found faithful unto my name at the last day, for he shall be lifted up to dwell in the kingdom prepared for him from the foundation of the world. And behold it is I that hath spoken it. Amen.

ETHER 4:18–19

Throughout the scriptures, the Lord uses striking contrasts to awaken our minds and to enrich our understanding of sacred truths. One such example is found in the words of the great prophet and general Mormon as he considered the awful state of the unrepentant Nephite nation in the final hours of its destruction. In utter sorrow, he characterized them as lacking in common courtesy and compassion; he observed that they "delight in everything save that which is good," that they were "without principle and past feeling" (see Moro. 9:16–20). They had consistently resisted the Lord's call to repentance, hardening their hearts and exponentially increasing in wickedness. As a result, Mormon sadly comments that he "cannot recommend them unto God lest he should smite me" (Moro. 9:21).

Then we read his tender words to his son Moroni, who has faithfully kept the commandments of the Lord: "But behold, my son, I recommend thee unto God, and I trust in Christ that thou wilt be saved" (Moro. 9:22). This brief interchange between a faithful father and son reminds us that the Lord will save us *from* our sins, but not *in* our sins.

The Lord's call to repentance is constant and urgent, and we hear its ongoing refrain throughout the pages of scripture from the mouths of prophets and from the Savior Himself. The promise to those who are faithful in heeding this call is quite breathtaking in its magnificence. Consider the words of King Benjamin: "And moreover, I would desire that ye should consider on the blessed and happy state of those that keep the commandments of God. For behold, they are blessed in all things, both temporal and spiritual; and if they hold out faithful to the end they are received into heaven, that thereby they may dwell with God in a state of never-ending happiness. O remember, remember that these things are true; for the Lord God hath spoken it" (Mosiah 2:41).

It is well to remember that prominent in this promise is the principle of remaining faithful, of enduring to the end: "If thou wilt do good, yea, and hold out faithful to the end, thou shalt be saved in the kingdom of God, which is the greatest of all the gifts of God; for there is no gift greater than the gift of salvation" (D&C 6:13).

> *The Lord's call to repentance is constant and urgent, and we hear its ongoing refrain throughout the pages of scripture from the mouths of prophets and from the Savior Himself.*

The Lord keeps all of His promises to those who are constant in heeding His call to repentance: "I, the Lord, am bound when ye do what I say; but when ye do not what I say, ye have no promise" (D&C 82:10).

❧

"O love the Lord, all ye his saints: for the Lord preserveth the faithful, and plentifully rewardeth the proud doer" (Ps. 31:23).

REJOICE IN CHRIST

And we talk of Christ, we rejoice in Christ, we preach of Christ, we prophesy of Christ, and we write according to our prophecies, that our children may know to what source they may look for a remission of their sins.

2 NE. 25:26

While some may not think it "fashionable" to talk of Christ, or to look to Him for guidance, or to acknowledge His divinity, the scriptures are priceless and reassuring in their message that He is indeed our Savior, the Son of God, whose "work and glory" is "to bring to pass the immortality and eternal life of man" (Moses 1:39). Certainly this is a topic worthy of discussion. Thus it behooves us to follow Nephi's eloquent admonition—to talk of Him, to rejoice in Him, and to study and share the scriptures.

We are always more comfortable when talking about something about which we know a great deal. In talking of Christ, then, it is well for us to know a great deal about Him. The scriptures are, of course, our greatest source of information on this sacred topic. The Savior very plainly states the purpose of our scripture study: "Search the scriptures; for in them ye think ye have eternal life: and they are they which testify of me" (John 5:39).

The prophet Lehi's sons, under their father's direction and on an errand from the Lord, went to great lengths at significant personal danger to secure the brass plates in order to have the scriptures to study and share with ensuing generations of their children. We do not have these types of obstacles to overcome—the scriptures are readily accessible worldwide in numerous languages; our challenge is to open them and search them and then open our mouths in Christ-centered conversations with family and friends.

In a general conference address, Elder D. Todd Christofferson spoke insightfully about the main purpose of scripture, which is to fill us with faith in our Heavenly Father and His Beloved Son, to guide us in knowing Them and loving Them, to prepare us for eternal life. "And this is life eternal, that they might know thee the only true God, and Jesus Christ, whom thou hast sent" (John 17:3) (see "The Blessing of Scripture," *Ensign*, May 2010, 34).

> *The more we learn and talk of the Savior, the more reasons we find to rejoice in Him.*

The more we learn and talk of the Savior, the more reasons we find to rejoice in Him. The Apostle Paul admonishes us to "Rejoice in the Lord alway: and again I say, Rejoice" (Philip. 4:4). We rejoice that He is our Elder Brother, that He is our Savior who wrought the great and infinite Atonement in our behalf, that He is our merciful Mediator with the Father. We rejoice that He knows us and loves us and that He longs to hold us in the arms of His love. We rejoice in His great plan of happiness; we rejoice in His birth and earthly ministry; we rejoice in the Restoration of His everlasting gospel. Consider the joyful words of the Psalmist: "But let all those that put their trust in thee rejoice: let them ever shout for joy, because thou defendest them: let them also that love thy name be joyful in thee" (Ps. 5:11).

❧

"Rejoice, the Lord is King!" (Hymns, no. 66).

The Lord's Purposes and His Promise

For the eternal purposes of the Lord shall roll on, until all the promises shall be fulfilled.

Morm. 8:22

In all dispensations, there has been opposition to the Lord's work and purposes. The avowed purpose of Satan and his hosts is to frustrate the work of the Lord—to "breathe out wrath and strifes against the work of the Lord, and against the covenant people of the Lord who are the house of Israel." They seek to destroy the work of the Lord so that He "will not remember his covenant which he hath made unto the house of Israel" (see Morm. 8:21).

Despite their unholy attempts to destroy and nullify God's purposes and His people, and in spite of temporary victories, Satan and his minions have proved wholly unsuccessful in their efforts.

A portion of Adam's posterity strayed from the truths of the gospel, but those who remained faithful were favored of the Lord, and from them came righteous generations. The majority of the people in Noah's time loved wickedness more than righteousness, but the Lord in His mercy saved a righteous portion of His people. The Israelites who came out of Egypt erred in keeping God's laws, but in due and refining time became the chastened children of Israel who were worthy to receive the promises of the Lord. A righteous remnant of a wicked nation taken captive returned to their homeland and rebuilt the temple in Jerusalem. The members of a fledgling Church restored by the Lord through His prophet in these latter days were hounded and driven and persecuted, but those who faithfully withstood these persecutions put their trust in the Lord and their feet on the path of faith.

We read that "For this purpose the Son of God was manifested, that he might destroy the works of the devil" (1 Jn. 3:8). The Lord's purposes cannot be derailed. "His purposes fail not, neither are there any who can stay his hand" (D&C 76:3).

The words *eternal* and *roll* are particularly meaningful in this scripture. We are assured that God never changes His mind or His plans or His promises, and that there is an ongoing impetus that cannot

> *The Lord's purposes cannot be derailed.*

be stopped by any means or force. Other people may disappoint us by their lack of fidelity, but our Father in Heaven and His Son are true and unchanging in their purposes and promises—and the promises are indeed glorious. We read in the epistle of James, "Hearken, my beloved brethren, Hath not God chosen the poor of this world rich in faith, and heirs of the kingdom which he hath promised to them that love him?" (James 2:5). The Apostle Paul tells us that the greatest of God's promises is the "hope of eternal life, which God, that cannot lie, promised before the world began" (Titus 1:2). God is most assuredly our "mighty fortress, a tower of strength ne'er failing," who "overcometh all" (*Hymns*, no. 68).

❧

"For he remembereth his holy promise, and Abraham his servant" (Ps. 105:42).

A Marvelous Work and a Wonder

Therefore, I will proceed to do a marvelous work among this people, yea, a marvelous work and a wonder, for the wisdom of their wise and learned shall perish, and the understanding of their prudent shall be hid.

2 Ne. 27:26

The gospel of Jesus Christ as restored in its fullness in these latter days is truly the marvelous work and wonder promised by the Lord. That a young, unlearned farm boy would be the Lord's chosen instrument in bringing to pass this promise is wondrous in and of itself, but is a fact that often proves to be a stumbling block to those who consider themselves wise in the ways of the world and learned in the eyes of men. Yet Joseph Smith took the Lord at His word after reading in James 1:5 that God would bestow His wisdom on anyone who asked for it with unwavering faith. As a result, wisdom was bestowed on Joseph in its purest and highest form. Joseph's earnest, faith-filled, and heartfelt prayer set the stage for the Restoration of the gospel of Jesus Christ and for the coming forth of the Book of Mormon, another testament of Jesus Christ.

During the course of Joseph Smith's mortal life, he was loved and hated with equal intensity. Those who humbly sought to know whether he spoke the truth received their own witness and wisdom from the Lord, while those who cast their lot on the side of doubt and skepticism hardened their hearts and closed their minds and ears to the whisperings of the Spirit, their own spirits darkened in murderous fury. Joseph Smith was martyred, and the detractors of the Lord's work thought they had silenced his voice and his testimony forever—indeed, they thought they had silenced the voice of God, refusing in their narrow and closed minds to let Him speak once again to His children. Yet the marvelous works and wonders of the Lord continue to roll forth as the stone that "became a great mountain, and filled the earth" (Dan. 2:35).

The Book of Mormon, translated by the Prophet Joseph Smith by the power of God, continues to be the pure word of God, "the keystone of our religion" ("Introduction," the Book of Mormon). It contains wisdom that encompasses and surpasses that of any who claim to be wise and learned and

> *The gospel of Jesus Christ as restored in its fullness in these latter days is truly the marvelous work and wonder promised by the Lord.*

prudent. It has truly filled the earth with its eternal truths. As a companion testament with the Holy Bible, its pages contain all the coursework we require in order to qualify for spiritual "graduate work" in God's kingdom. No wonder it is a "wonder."

Well might we joyfully proclaim,
"The glorious gospel light has shone
 In this the latter day
With such intelligence that none
From truth need turn away" (*Hymns*, no. 283).

"I shall proceed to do a marvelous work among them . . . that I may set my hand again the second time to recover my people"
(2 Ne. 29:1).

THE GIFT OF THE HOLY GHOST

And they did pray for that which they most desired; and they desired that the Holy Ghost should be given unto them.

3 NE. 19:9

We are admonished to seek earnestly "the best gifts, always remembering for what they are given" (D&C 46:8). Among all the gifts of God, the gift of the Holy Ghost is one we should desire above all others. Elder Bruce R. McConkie tells us that it is the greatest of all of God's gifts, and that as we embrace this gift during mortality, we have the promise of an eternal inheritance (see *The Mortal Messiah* [Salt Lake City: Deseret Book, 1980] 2:122).

The gift of the Holy Ghost is a gift freely and graciously given to all who enter the waters of baptism, but it is a gift that must be cherished and nourished. In the presence of the Savior, His Apostles on this continent expressed an earnest and heartfelt desire to receive the Holy Ghost, a prayer that was speedily answered because they had offered the Savior their gift of broken hearts and contrite spirits (see 3 Ne. 9:20). We must offer the Lord the same gift if we are to receive and enjoy the blessings of the gift of the Holy Ghost.

A broken heart and a contrite spirit are the evidences of true humility; it is offering our "whole souls as an offering unto him" (Omni 1:26). "The sacrifices of God are a broken spirit: a broken and a contrite heart, O God, thou wilt not despise" (Ps. 51:17). In the process, we surrender all our sins, not just a portion of them.

Elder Bruce C. Hafen counsels us that lip service alone will not suffice. If our outward words and actions belie a heart that is set on worldly pursuits and aspirations and distractions, then we cannot truly offer that heart to God. We are, in essence, hiding our heart from God rather than giving it to Him (see *The Broken Heart* [Salt Lake City: Deseret Book, 1989], 122–123).

What are the returns on this personal spiritual investment? The Savior promises us that as we receive and accept the gift of the Holy Ghost, we will experience comfort and peace, we will be taught all things, and we will have a remembrance of all things spiritual (see John 14:26). The Holy Ghost will testify of the Savior, that we too may gain a sure testimony of Him (see John 15:26); the Holy Ghost will "reprove the world of sin," thus reassuring us that good will triumph over evil (see John 16:26). Nephi tells us that this great gift enables us to "speak with the tongue of angels, and shout praises unto the Holy One of Israel" (2 Ne. 31:13); we will not hesitate to express our gratitude and to share our testimonies.

> *Among all the gifts of God, the gift of the Holy Ghost is one we should desire above all others.*

It is by the power of the Holy Ghost that we are able to confess that Jesus is the Christ (see Moro. 7:44). We are also promised that "If [we] will enter in by the way and receive the Holy Ghost, it will show unto [us] all things what [we] should do" (2 Ne. 32:5). Paul declares that "The kingdom of God is . . . righteousness, and peace, and joy in the Holy Ghost" (Rom. 14:17). These are indeed magnificent promises and blessings inherent with receiving the gift of the Holy Ghost.

❦

"The love of God is shed abroad in our hearts by the Holy Ghost which is given unto us" (Rom. 5:5).

ACKNOWLEDGING THE SAVIOR

Yea, every knee shall bow, and every tongue confess before him. Yea, even at the last day, when all men shall stand to be judged of him, then shall they confess that he is God.

MOSIAH 27:31

This scripture is a very personal reminder of our individual privilege and responsibility to humbly witness and confess that Jesus is the Christ. Our bended knees signify our acknowledgment of, our respect and gratitude for, and our loyalty to heavenly royalty.

The pattern for our personal acknowledgment is found throughout the scriptures. Moses spoke face to face with the Lord and rebuked Satan, who tempted him to forsake his marvelous spiritual experience. Moses's answer constituted his testimony: "Depart from me, Satan, for this one God only will I worship, which is the God of glory" (Moses 1:20).

Job declared in the extremity of his suffering, "For I know that my redeemer liveth, and that he shall stand at the latter day upon the earth" (Job 19:25). There was no doubt, no fear, no hesitation—only a sure and humble and strong testimony and acknowledgment of the Savior.

The prophet Lehi testified to his family and to all who would subsequently read and be comforted and strengthened by these glorious words: "I have beheld his glory, and I am encircled about eternally in the arms of his love" (2 Ne. 1:15).

Mary, the mother of Christ, was a special witness of her Son's humble birth, His miraculous ministry, His agonizing death, and His glorious Resurrection. The scriptures tell us that Mary "kept all these things, and pondered them in her heart"

(Luke 2:19). She received many witnesses of Her Son's mission and divinity and remained true to them all.

The Savior Himself bears personal record and testimony of His mission and His identity: "Behold, I am Jesus Christ the Son of God. . . . I am the light and the life of the world. I am Alpha and Omega, the beginning and the end" (3 Ne. 9:15, 18).

God the Father also bears testimony to the identity and mission of His Son and of His personal love and approval of Him: "Behold my Beloved Son, in whom I am well pleased . . . hear ye him" (3 Ne. 11:7). As we "hear Him," we come on bended knee to believe Him, love Him, trust Him, ac-

> *Our bended knees signify our acknowledgment of, our respect and gratitude for, and our loyalty to heavenly royalty.*

cept Him, follow Him, and openly and joyfully confess Him.

Oh Savior,
I live for the day
When every knee shall bow.
As I kneel, let me hear
All creation proclaim thy divinity.
But let us not wait
For that glad day.
Rather, give us the wisdom
To live that moment
Today (Audrey Megerian, "Let Us Not Wait," *Ensign*, Jan. 1988).

"Fear God, and give glory to him who sitteth upon the throne, forever and ever; for the hour of his judgment is come"
(D&C 88:104).

Faith unto Repentance

And thus he shall bring salvation to all those who shall believe on his name; this being the intent of this last sacrifice, to bring about the bowels of mercy, which overpowereth justice, and bringeth about means unto men that they may have faith unto repentance. And thus mercy can satisfy the demands of justice, and encircles them in the arms of safety, while he that exercises no faith unto repentance is exposed to the whole law of the demands of justice; therefore only unto him that has faith unto repentance is brought about the great and eternal plan of redemption.

ALMA 34:15–16

The Prophet Joseph Smith taught that "Salvation could not come to the world without the mediation of Jesus Christ" (*Teachings of the Prophet Joseph Smith* [Salt Lake City: Deseret Book, 1976], 323). His mediation is a manifestation of His mercy, and His supreme mercy was manifested through His great atoning sacrifice, a gift of infinite love extended to every child of God. We must have faith that through His Atonement we can be made spiritually clean and whole. This is the quality of faith that motivates us to true and sincere repentance—which, by the Lord's definition, means that we "will confess [our sins] and forsake them" (D&C 58:43).

"Faith unto repentance" means that we put forth our very best efforts and that we do not procrastinate the day of our repentance. Examples of procrastination taken to an extreme are evident in the scriptures; we are reminded of the people in Noah's day who were repeatedly warned and were then destroyed by the flood. Our procrastination is usually more gradual and subtle, but when we become too comfortable and delay or deny the repentance process, we also deny ourselves the comforting mercies of the Atonement.

We have all witnessed in the media the miraculous rescues of people who jump from burning buildings into safety nets. In very simplistic terms, the Atonement is our "safety net," put in place by our loving and gracious Savior to save us from the Fall and from our personal falls from grace. The Savior has promised us that there need be no moments of doubt if we have faith unto repentance: "Be faithful and diligent in keeping the commandments of God, and I will encircle thee in the arms of my love" (D&C 6:20). Nephi bears testimony of this

> *"faith unto repentance" means that we put forth our very best efforts in overcoming our shortcomings.*

principle when he says, "the Lord hath redeemed my soul from hell; I have beheld his glory, and I am encircled about eternally in the arms of his love" (2 Ne. 1:15).

Salvation is promised to all who will repent and accept the saving grace of Jesus Christ. His promise is sure, and His words remind us of just what a precious gift this is. "If thou wilt do good, yea, and hold out faithful to the end, thou shalt be saved in the kingdom of God, which is the greatest of all the gifts of God; for there is no gift greater than the gift of salvation" (D&C 6:13).

∽⚬

"The Lord is my light and my salvation; whom then shall I fear?" (Ps. 27:1).

FORGIVENESS

And it came to pass that I did frankly forgive them all that they had done, and I did exhort them that they would pray unto the Lord their God for forgiveness. And it came to pass that they did so.

1 NE. 7:21

The word that stands out most prominently in this scripture is the word *frankly*, which carries with it a connotation of forthrightness and sincerity. In family situations it is often difficult to let go of grudges and separate the sin from the sinner. We have high expectations of those with whom we are close and with whom we share or wish to share a loving relationship. When that closeness and love is violated, we are often tempted to nurse the hurt and let it fester and grow to even greater proportions.

Nephi had been wronged by his brothers in ways that, thankfully, most of us will never experience. Who could have blamed him for withholding his forgiveness? The answer, of course, is the Lord. Nephi's forgiveness was a Christlike and candid response that emanated from a genuine concern for the welfare of his rebellious brothers' souls. There were no strings attached, no rehearsals of the list of their crimes against him, no verbal reprisals or recriminations, no dire threats about what they could expect in the form of punishment from the Lord. In his brief words we hear only an exhortation for them to also seek the Lord's cleansing and healing forgiveness.

The Savior is clear in His teachings regarding our need to forgive one another: "I, the Lord, will forgive whom I will forgive, but of you it is required to forgive all men" (D&C 64:10). Note the inclusiveness of the word *all*.

President Spencer W. Kimball recalls the example of President George Albert Smith, whose buggy robe was stolen and whose response was one of solicitous concern rather than anger. He simply wished to find the person responsible and offer him an additional warm blanket and food as well (see *The Miracle of Forgiveness* [Salt Lake City: Bookcraft, 1969], 284). It is our obligation to forgive so that "old grievances will be forgiven and forgotten, enemies will become friends again, skeletons will be buried, and the closet of dry bones will be locked and the key thrown away" (*Miracle of Forgiveness*, 282).

A simple poem by Sara Teasdale captures the essence of true forgiveness:

> *In family situations it is often difficult to let go of grudges and separate the sin from the sinner.*

Let it be forgotten, as a flower is forgotten,
Forgotten as a fire that once was singing gold,
Let it be forgotten forever and ever,
Time is a kind friend, he will make us old.
If anyone asks, say it was forgotten
Long and long ago,
As a flower, as a fire, as a hushed footfall
In a long forgotten snow (*A Treasury of Poems*, comp. Sarah Anne Stuart [New York: Galahad Books, 1996], 653).

"I, the Lord, will forgive whom I will forgive, but of you it is required to forgive all men" (D&C 64:10).

PATINCE IN AFFLICTIONS

And now my beloved brethren, I would exhort you to have patience. . . . and bear with those afflictions, with a firm hope that ye shall one day rest from all your afflictions.

ALMA 34:40–41

While patience in adversity is often thought of as a passive trait, it actually requires great faith and trust in the Lord's watchful care. Elder Neal A. Maxwell defined patience as "a willingness, in a sense, to watch the unfolding purposes of God with a sense of wonder and awe—rather than pacing up and down within the cell of our circumstance" (*The Neal A. Maxwell Quote Book* [Salt Lake City: Bookcraft, 1997], 241). It is well to remember that all things will be made right in the Lord's good time, and that no matter how tough our difficulties seem now, they will be but a small moment in the eternal scheme of things.

The refining fire of affliction is just that—a refining process, an opportunity for us to grow and progress, even though that process can be painful and take us way out of our comfort zone. Only after we have passed through pain or sorrow or fear do we look back and see the Lord's wisdom, love, and constant companionship.

Enduring our afflictions with patience brings a renewal of faith in the Savior and a more sure knowledge of His love and His desire to strengthen and lift us. He promises His rest to those who are patient and faithful: "Come unto me all ye that labour and are heavy laden, and I will give you rest" (Matt. 11:28).

C. S. Lewis drew a remarkable analogy between the remodeling of the human soul and the remodeling of a house: "Imagine yourself as a living house. God comes in to rebuild that house. At first, perhaps, you can understand what He is doing. He is getting the drains right and stopping the leaks in the roof and so on: you knew that those jobs needed doing and so you are not surprised. But presently, He starts knocking the house about in a way that hurts abominably and does not seem to make sense. What on earth is He up to? The explanation is that He is building quite a different house from the one you thought of—throwing out a new wing here, putting on an extra floor there, running

> *All things will be made right in the Lord's good time, and our difficulties will be but a small moment in the eternal scheme.*

up towers, making courtyards. You thought you were going to be made into a decent little cottage: but He is building a palace" (*Mere Christianity* [New York: Macmillan, 1960], 174).

As we look back on our adversities, may our declarations of faith and patience be like those of Alma: "And I have been supported under trials and troubles of every kind, yea, and in all manner of afflictions; yea, God has delivered me from prison, and from bonds, and from death; yea, and I do put my trust in him, and he will still deliver me" (Alma 36:27).

"Rest in the Lord, and wait patiently for him" (Ps. 37:7).

The Lord's Directions Are Clear

O my son, do not let us be slothful because of the easiness of the way; for so it was with our fathers; for so it was prepared for them, that if they would look they might live; even so it is with us. The way is prepared, and if we will look we may live forever. . . . yea, see that ye look to God and live.

Alma 37:46–47

When the children of Israel were afflicted with poisonous flying serpents, the Lord directed Moses to make a serpent of brass and raise it on a pole so that anyone who was bitten could simply look at the brass serpent and be physically healed. This, of course, was a type or symbol of the Savior being lifted up, "That whosoever believeth in him should not perish, but have eternal life" (John 3:15). When we look to God, our spirits are strengthened and healed, and we are infused with spiritual power.

Perhaps it is easy for us to become casual in our scripture study and thus miss the opportunity to become well and intimately acquainted with our Savior. We have so many responsibilities and obligations that cry out for our time and attention that we sometimes forget to be about our Father's business.

Elder Carlos E. Asay cautions us about taking the scriptures for granted. He points out that we meticulously remember and keep our appointments with doctors and dentists, while sometimes forgetting and neglecting or even failing to make appointments with our scriptures. We all too easily forget that the scriptures enable us to hear God's voice and receive His clear directions (see "Look to God and Live," *Ensign*, Nov. 1978).

Mortality is but a moment compared to the promise of everlasting life. However, it is what we do while in this mortal state that determines the quality of our eternal reward. If our ultimate goal is to enjoy the privilege of the Savior's presence, then it would be well for us to know Him. We are far more comfortable associating with friends than with strangers or mere acquaintances. The Lord desires to be our friend: "I will call you friends, for you are my friends, and ye shall have an inheritance with me" (D&C 93:45). Notice that He did not say we are His *acquaintances*. Let us cultivate that intimate friendship by knowing Him and deserving His gracious compliment.

Look to God and live. The way is easy, and the directions are clear. "Behold, I am the law, and the light. Look unto me, and endure to the end, and ye shall live; for unto him that endureth to the end will I give eternal life" (3 Ne. 15:9).

> *Mortality is but a moment compared to the promise of everlasting life. However, it is what we do while in this mortal state that determines the quality of our eternal reward.*

❧

"And now, I would commend you to seek this Jesus of whom the prophets and apostles have written, that the grace of God the Father, and also the Lord Jesus Christ, and the Holy Ghost, which beareth record of them, may be and abide in you forever. Amen"
(Ether 12:41).

BAPTISMAL COVENANT

And it came to pass that he said unto them: Behold, here are the waters of Mormon (for thus were they called) and now, as ye are desirous to come into the fold of God, and to be called his people, and are willing to bear one another's burdens, that they may be light; Yea, and are willing to mourn with those that mourn; yea, and comfort those that stand in need of comfort, and to stand as witnesses of God at all times and in all things, and in all places that ye may be in, even until death, that ye may be redeemed of God, and be numbered with those of the first resurrection, that ye may have eternal life.

MOSIAH 18:8–9

Baptism is a sacred covenant—an agreement between us and God in which we promise to honor the terms He has set. Thus, our baptismal covenant is an ongoing process rather than an event. We promise to help each other with difficulties—not to be too busy with our own burdens, assuming and hoping that someone else will pick up the slack. We promise to be compassionate and comforting to those who have cause to mourn—not just for a few hours or days, but for as long as we are needed in that capacity. When someone experiences the death of a loved one, we are easily and willingly caught up in the outward expressions of compassion—meals, flowers, cleaning, and warm hugs. But as time goes by, we need to remember that hearts are still wounded and tender, and act accordingly.

We promise that we will stand as witnesses of Christ—and Alma's words are very pointed in this regard—"in all places that ye may be in" (Mosiah 18:9). There is no room for a double standard—one for Sunday and church, and another for the other days and places. With the Apostle Paul, we too should be able to say that we are "not ashamed of the gospel of Christ" (Rom. 1:16), nor should we ever give the Lord any reason to be ashamed of us.

Each Sunday we have the privilege to renew this sacred covenant as we take the sacrament. As we ponder the words of the sacramental prayers, our thoughts are turned to a remembrance of our Exemplar, and we review how we are doing and recommit ourselves to doing better in order to constantly have the Lord's Spirit as our companion.

> *Baptism is a sacred covenant—an agreement between us and God in which we promise to honor the terms He has set.*

If we are faithful to our baptismal covenant, the Lord on His part promises us that we will come forth in the First Resurrection, or the Resurrection of the Just, which will take place at His Second Coming. Then we will be blessed to receive a celestial glory. "For thus saith the Lord—I, the Lord, am merciful and gracious . . . and delight to honor those who serve me in righteousness and in truth unto the end. Great shall be their reward and eternal shall be their glory" (D&C 76:5–6).

"We now repent of all our sin
And come with broken heart,
And to thy covenant enter in
And choose the better part" (Hymns, no. 180).

Small and Simple Things

But behold I say unto you, that by small and simple things are great things brought to pass; and small means in many instances doth confound the wise.

Alma 37:6

When Naaman, captain of the hosts of the king of Syria, discovered that he had the dreaded disease of leprosy, he sought a miraculous cure from the prophet Elisha. When Elisha sent word for Naaman to wash in the River Jordan seven times, Naaman was both insulted and enraged. He turned away disdainfully until his servant convinced him that he had nothing to lose by following Elisha's instructions. And sure enough—it worked. A small and simple act produced a miraculous cure.

A small, round ball of "curious workmanship" (1 Ne. 16:10) appeared outside Lehi's tent as he and his family sojourned in the wilderness. When the family members exercised faith and obedience, the two spindles on the ball pointed them in the right direction. A small and simple compass made what seemed like an impossible journey a reality.

On April 6, 1839, a small group of approximately fifty people met in the log house of Peter Whitmer Sr. in New York for the purpose of organizing The Church of Jesus Christ of Latter-day Saints. From that small group, the Church has swelled in ranks to well more than 14 million people worldwide. From a small and simple act of faith and obedience, a marvelous work and a wonder continues to unfold.

On March 27, 1836, the Kirtland Temple—the first temple built in this dispensation—was dedicated. There are now well more than one hundred temples in operation throughout the world, with dozens pending.

We may consider these profound examples far removed from our own personal experiences, but the Lord sees and appreciates all of our small and simple efforts—small, selfless acts of service; quiet and loving acts of kindness; a smile offered to a stranger that lifts and lightens a heavy heart; a simple and sincere compliment to a child or spouse that reminds them that they are loved and valuable; the benefit of the doubt given to someone when others are quick to condemn. All of these have eternal significance and relevance to God's eternal purposes.

Emily Dickinson says it well in her poem, "If I Can Stop One Heart from Breaking"—

> *The Lord sees and appreciates all of our small and simple efforts.*

> If I can stop one heart from breaking,
> I shall not live in vain;
> If I can ease one life the aching,
> Or cool one pain,
> Or help one lonely person
> Into happiness again
> I shall not live in vain

(*A Treasury of Poems*, comp. Sarah Anne Stuart [New York: Galahad Books, 1996], 57).

"You know, brethren, that a very large ship is benefited very much by a very small helm in the time of a storm" (*D&C* 123:16).

THE PLAN OF HAPPINESS

O how great the plan of our God! For on the other hand, the paradise of God must deliver up the spirits of the righteous, and the grave deliver up the body of the righteous; and the spirit and the body is restored to itself again, and all men become incorruptible, and immortal, and they are living souls, having a perfect knowledge like unto us in the flesh, save it be that our knowledge shall be perfect.

2 NE. 9:13

In a world where many question whether there is a God, much less continued existence beyond the grave, how blessed we are to have a knowledge of God's love and of His great plan of happiness for us both here and in the eternities. It is incomprehensible to think that God would send us down to earth without a plan for our return to Him. We most definitely were sent on this vital journey with a round-trip ticket.

In today's uncertain economy, we can never count on paying the same price for an airline ticket, nor can we always expect to fill our gas tanks at reasonable and stable rates. There is one journey, however, for which the price is fixed and reasonable, for which the rules of travel are clearly spelled out. In the grand premortal council, we eagerly looked forward to our travel opportunities, and while the journey would involve a brief separation from our Father's presence, we were assured that our Savior would pay the price for our return trip.

While the bodies we so eagerly desired for the mortal phase of our journey would be subject to the ravages of illness and aging, the return-trip plan promises us that they will be restored to their prime condition (see Alma 40:23). This, of course, is made possible through the Savior's Resurrection, an integral and glorious portion of our "ticket," with no expense on our part—no fine print and no hidden clauses.

And as if that were not gift enough, the Father gave His Son as a willing sacrifice to atone for our sins so that our spirits would be clean and whole as well. There is, however, some fine print in *this* portion of our "ticket." We are expected to use our mortal probation wisely, to repent of our sins.

We can offer no less than our best effort to Him that took upon Himself *all* of our sorrows, sins, and imperfections, so that we could return to Their presence through the principle of repentance.

> *Through the Savior's infinite, divine, and comprehensive Atonement, we can anticipate the blessings of a joyous return to our Father's and Savior's presence.*

The return-trip ticket is available to all of God's children. There are no exclusions of age, race, or gender. Regardless of their dates of travel, everyone will have the opportunity to receive the blessings of the great plan of happiness. In His love and mercy, the Savior makes it possible for those who wait in paradise to hear the good news of the gospel—to receive, as it were, their "final boarding pass."

"And now, behold, I say unto you: This is the plan of salvation unto all men, through the blood of mine Only Begotten, who shall come in the meridian of time" (Moses 6:62; emphasis added).

HUMILITY AND OBEDIENCE

And if men come unto me I will show unto them their weakness. I give unto men weakness that they may be humble; and my grace is sufficient for all men that humble themselves before me; for if they humble themselves before me, and have faith in me, then will I make weak things become strong unto them.

ETHER 12:27

As the Lord points out in this scripture, we all have weaknesses that can be turned into strengths; however, it is only as we turn to the Savior for guidance that He helps us become aware of what those weaknesses are.

When Moses took the two new tablets of stone and went up unto Mount Sinai to receive the law, the Lord spoke with him and made promises regarding the children of Israel, the fulfillment of which were entirely dependent on their obedience. Through the voice of His prophets, the Lord has made great promises to all of His children in all dispensations, including those of us privileged to live in these latter days. And the conditions of fulfillment are the same for us as they were for the children of Israel or any other of God's children in any other dispensation. Obedience is the key that unlocks the door to the Lord's promised blessings, and it is humility that motivates obedience.

Humility allows us to have faith in the Lord and to be taught by Him, thereby increasing our spiritual strength. The prophet Jacob tells us that the Lord shows us our weakness to remind us that it is only through His grace that we can become strong. "Nevertheless, the Lord God showeth us our weakness that we may know that it is by his grace, and his great condescensions unto the children of men, that we have power to do these things" (Jacob 4:7).

We see a daily fulfillment of this in the missionaries called to preach the gospel in all parts of the world. The majority of them are young and inexperienced in the ways of the world and in gospel knowledge; they often struggle to learn a foreign language; their formal college education has just begun; and their experience in human relationships is very basic. But through their faith, obedience, and humility, these "weak things" become strong in all the ways that truly count. The Lord is able to teach them, and in turn they are able to teach the things of the

> *It is only as we turn to the Savior for guidance that He helps us become aware of our weaknesses.*

Spirit, "that the fulness of my gospel might be proclaimed by the weak and the simple unto the ends of the world, and before kings and rulers" (D&C 1:23). It is as the Apostle Paul said, "But God hath chosen the foolish things of the world to confound the wise; and God hath chosen the weak things of the world to confound the things which are mighty" (1 Cor. 1:27).

Our strength comes through humbly learning and doing the will of the Lord, relying always on His grace. "Therefore shall you keep all the commandments which I command you this day, that ye may be strong" (Deut. 11:8).

❧

"The fear of the Lord is the instruction of wisdom; and before honour is humility" (Prov. 15:33).

THE LIGHT OF CHRIST

For behold, my brethren, it is given unto you to judge, that ye may know good from evil; and the way to judge is as plain, that ye may know with a perfect knowledge, as the daylight is from the dark night. For behold, the Spirit of Christ is given to every man, that he may know good from evil; wherefore, I show unto you the way to judge; for every thing which inviteth to do good, and to persuade to believe in Christ, is sent forth by the power and gift of Christ; wherefore ye may know with a perfect knowledge it is of God.

MORO. 7:15–16

Courtroom dramas regularly unfold in the news and defendants are judged as to their guilt or innocence. As bystanders, we are often left to wonder how accurate and just these judgments are and how much of the verdict has been based on the machinations of clever lawyers and skewed perceptions.

But we need not depend on such unreliable variables. There is one unerring source that can guarantee a just and true verdict in all our judgments—it is the Light of Christ: "For the word of the Lord is truth, and whatsoever is truth is light, and whatsoever is light is Spirit, even the Spirit of Jesus Christ. And the Spirit giveth light to every man that cometh into the world; and the Spirit enlighteneth every man through the world, that hearkeneth to the voice of the Spirit" (D&C 84:45–46). While we should not confuse the Light of Christ with the Holy Ghost, it is well for us to understand that the Light of Christ certainly prepares us to perceive and receive that great and significant gift as well.

We are constantly in the process of making decisions and judgments, some more crucial than others. On a very basic level we must decide what we will wear and what we will eat; on a higher level, we must decide what we will watch, what we will read, how we will fulfill our Church callings, how we will receive the pleasing word of God from our leaders. The Lord expects us to use our common sense, but even that is guided by His light, which He expects us to use well and wisely.

As we make our judgments, we either magnify or diminish this Light. Each righteous decision and judgment is guided by the full power of Christ's light, while every unjust and unwise judgment is tantamount to subjecting that light to a "dimmer" switch. The degree to which the Light of

> *Enabled and ennobled by the Light of Christ, we can bring in the true and correct verdict in all our judgments.*

Christ illuminates our lives increases or decreases in direct proportion to our efforts to become, as Moroni said, "true followers of . . . Jesus Christ," and "be purified even as he is pure" (Moro. 7:48). The Savior Himself affirms this principle: "That which is of God is light; and he that receiveth light, and continueth in God, receiveth more light; and that light grows brighter and brighter until the perfect day" (D&C 50:24).

Enabled and ennobled by the Light of Christ, we can bring in the true and correct verdict in all our judgments. There will be no shades of gray.

❧

"And whatsoever persuadeth men to do good is of me; for good cometh cometh of none save it be of me" (Ether 4:12).

123

Thoughts, Words, and Deeds

But this much I can tell you, that if ye do not watch your-selves, and your thoughts, and your words, and your deeds, and observe the commandments of God, and continue in the faith of what ye have heard concerning the coming of our Lord, even unto the end of your lives, ye must perish. And now, O man, remember, and perish not.

MOSIAH 4:30

This scripture makes it obvious that there is a reciprocal agreement among our thoughts, words, and deeds. Stated another way, each one produces a chain reaction. We watch in horror as earthquakes ravage various parts of the world—and close on the heels of these destructive and frightening earthquakes often follows an equally devastating tsunami. One triggers the other. And so it is with the way we think, speak, and act.

Alma the Younger clearly understood and taught this principle, reminding us that our words, works, and thoughts will condemn us (see Alma 12:14). Certainly this sinner turned prophet of God knew how true this is. As a young man, he threw himself wholeheartedly into apostate activities that had been thought out very carefully and discussed at some length with his friends before they came to fruition as works of darkness. Then when the Lord sent an angel with a restraining order, Alma had occasion and time to think and to remember his great sins; there followed a remembrance of his father's teachings concerning the Atonement. Alma subsequently declared his words of remorse and repentance, and then spent the remainder of his days in the service of God.

The Savior taught that every action, whether good or bad, begins with a thought: "Thefts, covetousness, wickedness, deceit, lasciviousness, an evil eye, blasphemy, pride, foolishness: All these evil things come from within, and defile the man" (Mark 7:22–23). Dishonesty in any form must first be contemplated before it becomes a "done deal." Likewise, as with the prophet Alma, our inner integrity is reflected in our words and actions.

The Greek philosopher Plato penned these words: "Beauty depends on simplicity—I mean the true simplicity of a rightly and nobly ordered mind and character. He is a fool who seriously inclines to weigh the beautiful by any other standard than that of the good. The good is the beautiful. Grant me to be beautiful in the inner man" (*The Republic*).

> *This scripture makes it obvious that there is a reciprocal agreement among our thoughts, words, and deeds.*

If we truly remember at all times to whom we look as our Exemplar—if our thoughts are Christ-oriented and Christ-centered—we achieve an inner beauty that produces a chain reaction in word and deed with pleasing eternal consequences.

"More holiness give me,
More strivings within,
More patience in suff'ring,
More sorrow for sin,
More faith in my Savior,
More sense of His care,
More joy in His service,
More purpose in prayer" (Hymns, no. 131).

GOOD WORKS

And see that ye have faith, hope, and charity, and then ye will always abound in good works.

ALMA 7:24

The three great virtues of faith, hope, and charity are rarely spoken of separately because they incrementally build on one another, with charity getting top billing. The Apostle Paul's memorable words verify this truth: "And now abideth faith, hope, and charity, these three; but the greatest of these is charity" (1 Cor. 13:13).

Charity is a virtue most often associated with good works. The Savior taught that "whosoever will lose his life for my sake, the same shall save it" (Luke 9:24), and that admonition has direct application to losing ourselves in the service of others.

Elder Dallin H. Oaks of the Quorum of the Twelve added his wise counsel on this topic in a conference talk. He cautions us against service that seeks the recognition and accolades of men—service that is motivated by selfishness rather than selflessness. He counsels us that it is only through service that is motivated by love of God and our fellow men that we qualify as recipients of God's promise of eternal life (see "Unselfish Service," *Ensign*, May, 2009, 95–96).

Consider the Savior's examples of service: He healed the sick, caused the blind to see, bade the cripples to walk, cast out evil spirits, raised the dead, loved and comforted the sinner, washed His Apostles' tired and dusty feet on the occasion of the Last Supper, reached out to His mother with His pure love in the last hours of His suffering on the cross, entrusted His mother into His beloved Apostle's care, and ultimately ransomed us all in Gethsemane and on Calvary.

Mother Teresa of Calcutta devoted her life to charity, to the selfless service and acts of love that reflected the Savior's example. Her words, found in a note on her bedside table when she died, remind us that our charity must be motivated solely by our desire to give rather than to receive: "People are unreasonable, illogical, and self-centered. Love them anyway. If you do good, people may accuse you of selfish motives. Do good

> *Charity is a virtue most often associated with good works, with deeds of unselfish service.*

anyway. If you are successful, you may win false friends and true enemies. Succeed anyway. The good you do may be forgotten tomorrow. Do good anyway. Honesty and openness make you vulnerable. Be honest and open anyway. What you spend years building may be destroyed overnight. Build anyway. People who really want help may attack you if you help them. Help them anyway. Give the world the best you have and you may get hurt. Give the world your best anyway."

"Have I done any good in the world today?
Have I helped anyone in need?
Have I cheered up the sad and made someone feel glad?
If not, I have failed indeed" (Hymns, no. 223).

Contention Is Contrary to the Lord's Spirit

For verily, verily I say unto you, he that hath the spirit of contention is not of me, but is of the devil, who is the father of contention, and he stirreth up the hearts of men to contend with anger, one with another. Behold, this is not my doctrine, to stir up the hearts of men, one against another; but this is my doctrine, that such things should be done away.

3 Ne. 11:29–30

It is interesting to note that this is one of the first things Jesus taught the Nephites following His appearance to them. After He had invited them to see and feel His wounds, He gave the prophet Nephi the power to baptize the people, and then spoke to them immediately about guarding against contention.

It is touching and significant to note the contrasts in this segment of scripture. The people have been moved to tears of joy and gratitude by the Lord's very presence and have expressed their love and adoration on bended knees at His feet: "Hosanna! Blessed be the name of the Most High God!" (3 Ne. 11:17). The Savior then cautions them against backsliding into the contentions—doctrinal and otherwise—that have "hitherto been the cause of their downfall." The Savior makes the source of contention crystal clear—it is of the devil, whose sole goal and purpose is to thwart the work of the Lord and alienate His people one from another and ultimately from the Savior.

The Lord is the Prince of Peace—and in contrast to the prince of darkness, who has always delighted in heart-hardening disputations that lead to disastrous eternal consequences, the Savior seeks to turn our hearts one to another in love, desiring to bestow an inner peace within us that leaves no room for anger, pride, or contention.

In the not-too-distant past, Jesus had spoken on this very matter to His Apostles in Jerusalem on the occasion of the Last Supper: "These things I have spoken unto you, that in me ye might have peace. In the world ye shall have tribulation: but be of good cheer; I have overcome the world" (John 16:33).

We have only to listen to news reports to know that contention is rampant in various parts of the world and that fear has a firm grasp on the hearts of many. Our mandate as disciples of the Lord Jesus Christ is to seek and cultivate in our personal lives, in our homes, and in all our relationships the peace that prevents prideful contentions. The Savior reiterates his stance on those who seek and radiate His peace: "And blessed are all the peacemakers, for they shall be called the children of God" (3 Ne. 12:9). The word *all* lets us know that His family is not a private and exclusive club. We are all invited to join, but the membership rules are clear: "Thou shalt love the Lord thy God with all thy heart, with all thy might, mind, and strength" and "thy neighbor as thyself" (D&C 59:5–6).

> *Our mandate as disciples of the Lord Jesus Christ is to cultivate the peace that prevents prideful contentions.*

⁓

"Thus did Alma teach his people, that every man should love his neighbor as himself, that there should be no contention among them" (Mosiah 23:15).

THE TESTIMONY OF PROPHETS

For, for this intent have we written these things, that they may know that we know of Christ, and we had a hope of his glory many hundred years before his coming; and not only we ourselves had a hope of his glory, but also all the holy prophets which were before us.

JACOB 4:4

The Book of Mormon was authored by God as He inspired His holy prophets, and it was written specifically for our time. Moroni bears witness of this truth: "Behold, I speak unto you as if ye were present, and yet ye are not. But behold, Jesus Christ hath shown you unto me, and I know your doing" (Morm. 8:35). As *Another Testament of Jesus Christ*, the purpose of this sacred record is to convince both "the Jew and Gentile that Jesus is the Christ, the Eternal God" (Title Page). Christ is the central focus of all scriptures, and prophets in all dispensations testify of Him that we might come to know and love and follow Him.

Nephi was privileged to see in vision the mortal Messiah as He ministered to the multitudes: "Behold the Lamb of God, yea, even the Son of the Eternal Father!" (1 Ne 11:21).

King Benjamin bore testimony of "Jesus Christ, the Son of God, the Father of heaven and earth" (Mosiah 3:8). Alma prophesies of Jesus' birth "at Jerusalem which is the land of our forefathers" (Alma 7:10). Helaman rehearses with his sons King Benjamin's testimony of the Savior: "Yea, remember that he cometh to redeem the world" (Hel. 5:9). The prophet Ether records Christ's personal witness to the brother of Jared: "Behold, I am Jesus Christ. I am the Father and the Son" (Ether 3:14).

The book of Isaiah resounds with Messianic testimony: "Behold, a virgin shall conceive, and bear a son, and shall call his name Immanuel" (Isa. 7:14). Jeremiah testifies, "Behold, the days come, saith the Lord, that I will raise unto David a righteous Branch, and a King shall reign and prosper, and shall execute judgment and justice in the earth" (Jer. 23:5).

Continuing in this sacred tradition and mission, modern prophets have also added their testimonies. Joseph Smith, the prophet who ushered in the dispensation of the fulness of times, bore this personal witness: "And this is the gospel, the glad tidings, which the voice out of the heavens bore record unto us— That he came into the world, even Jesus, to

> *Christ is the central focus of all scriptures, and prophets in all dispensations testify of Him.*

be crucified for the world, and to bear the sins of the world, and to sanctify the world, and to cleanse it from all unrighteousness; That through him all might be saved whom the Father had put into his power and made by him" (D&C 76:40–42). To that our beloved President Thomas S. Monson adds his personal witness that Jesus Christ is our living Savior, our gloriously resurrected Redeemer (see "He Is Not Here, but Is Risen," *Ensign*, April 2011, 5).

As we search the holy scriptures, our personal testimonies are strengthened, and our hope in Christ is renewed.

"Who is this King of glory? The Lord of hosts, he is the King of glory" (Ps. 24:10).

ASK, SEEK, KNOCK

Ask, and it shall be given unto you; seek, and ye shall find; knock, and it shall be opened unto you.

3 NE. 14:7

We might say that this scripture is a proactive formula for our interactions with the Lord. The words *ask*, *seek*, and *knock* are words that call for action and effort on our part, with a promise that our efforts faithfully and wisely expended will produce desirable results. It's like knowing the right combination to a lock.

The Lord does not recommend that we *tell* Him what we want, but rather that we *ask* for what we need. He also cautions us to be wise in our petitions: "Do not ask for that which you ought not" (D&C 8:10). Those of us with children are sometimes alarmed at what they ask for, knowing as parents that it would be unwise to acquiesce to their every wish, even when they are persistent.

It is the same when we ask amiss of the Lord. He tells us that our Heavenly Father knows what we really need and what will be good for us, and that our vain repetitions are not a successful way to get His attention—nor will they convince Him to fill our "orders" (see Matt. 6:7–8). Rather, He counsels us to "ask in faith, nothing wavering" (James 1:6), and to be contrite and obedient. Our appropriate petitions to the Lord will be granted in the Lord's time and in His infinite and loving wisdom.

The second part of the formula or combination is to *seek*. This is much different than the game of hide-and-seek that we all enjoyed as children. The Lord is not hiding, but can be found as we prayerfully and diligently search and ponder the scriptures; as we remember our daily prayers; as we give heed to ongoing revelations through His prophets; as we partake of the sacrament each week and renew our covenants with Him; as we attend the temple to serve and learn. The prophet Jeremiah reminds us, "And ye shall seek me, and find me, when ye shall search for me with all your heart" (Jer. 29:13). An occasional and random sampling of the scriptures, sporadic church and temple attendance, and a casual and optional attitude toward prayer just won't cut it.

Finally, we are invited to *knock*. This is the last element of the combination that assures the opening of a door. The Lord is not like the people who might ignore the knock on the door because they don't feel good or look good or just don't want to be disturbed. With the Lord, those are not options. When He tells us that He will open the door if we but knock, He means exactly what He is saying.

> *When He tells us that He will open the door if we but knock, He means exactly what He is saying.*

The figurative opening of the door is a literal promise of personal revelation. Windows and doors let in light, and the Lord's Light is synonymous with His glory. As the Lord opens His door to us, He shares His Light and glory and intelligence, and our minds and spirits are filled with truths needed for our personal progression.

"Seek the Lord, and his strength: seek his face evermore"
(Ps. 105:4).

APATHY

Therefore, wo be unto him that is at ease in Zion! Wo be unto him that crieth: All is well!

2 Ne. 28:24–2

There is something of a natural tendency in us to want to take things easy, to put on our rose-colored glasses and ignore the nooks and crannies in our spiritual lives that could bear much closer scrutiny. We all like to occasionally give ourselves a little pat on the back and tell ourselves that we're okay, especially when compared to someone else who doesn't seem quite as "okay" as we are. Why do something today that we could put off until tomorrow, especially when it comes to rousing ourselves spiritually? After all, who is going to come along with their white gloves and check for spiritual dust? If we dim the lights a little and pull the shades just a tad, our glance in the spiritual mirror tells us we're "lookin' good"!

However, deep down, we really know that some of those "nooks and crannies" could really use a little spit and polish. We can't afford to tell ourselves that, after all, we're not like so-and-so down the street who has a Word of Wisdom problem. Very often our own spiritual deficiencies are not quite so visible.

We may simply suffer from a condition that is known as *apathy*, which the Lord describes in vivid terms in the book of Revelation: "I know thy works, that thou art neither cold nor hot: I would thou wert cold or hot. So then because thou art lukewarm, and neither cold nor hot, I will spue thee out of my mouth" (Rev. 3:15–16).

There is nothing more disagreeable and disappointing than anticipating either a cold or hot drink and finding with the first sip that it is simply tepid. According to this scripture, it is equally disappointing to the Lord when our spiritual efforts and attitudes are just lukewarm. The Prophet Joseph Smith called it *a sleeping Christianity*, a condition that we must avoid "to enjoy the smiles of [our] Savior in these last days" (*Teachings of the Prophet Joseph Smith* [Salt Lake City: Deseret Book, 1976], 14). We need to be vigilant against the deadly disease of spiritual indifference.

Elder M. Russell Ballard cautions us that we may need to give ourselves a spiritual shake, to be proactive in our commitment to the Lord and intensely dedicated in our service to Him (see "How Is It with Us?" *Ensign*, May 2000).

> *If we dim the lights a little and pull the shades just a tad, our glance in the spiritual mirror tells us we're "lookin' good"!*

We cannot be indifferent to our need to do a bit of spiritual "spring cleaning." It is not enough to be a card-carrying member of The Church of Jesus Christ of Latter-day Saints; we must be vigilant about which aspects of our "cards" need to be renewed, which areas of our commitment need to be reviewed, and be up and doing—eagerly enrolling in "refresher courses" that keep us current in our eligibility for membership in God's kingdom.

≈

"Behold, this is your work, to keep my commandments, yea, with all your might, mind and strength" (D&C 11:20).

Spiritual Prosperity

And behold, all that he requires of you is to keep his commandments; and he has promised you that if ye would keep his commandments ye should prosper in the land; and he never doth vary from that which he hath said; therefore, if ye do keep his commandments he doth bless you and prosper you.

Mosiah 2:22

This scripture is a refrain we find repeated over and over in the pages of the Book of Mormon—so it must be as important for us in our day as it was for those in ancient times. It was the Lord's promise to Lehi and his family as they left the comforts of their life in Jerusalem and set out on a journey toward a destination known only to the Lord. Those members of Lehi's family who took the Lord at His word found that it was not an empty promise; they prospered both temporally and spiritually in their new promised land. And those who chose to skate on the thin ice of disobedience also found that the Lord was as good as His word.

The rules are simple, and they never change. They apply to all of God's children, regardless of where or when we live. The most exciting part of the Lord's promise is the spiritual prosperity we enjoy as a result of our obedience: "And, if you keep my commandments and endure to the end you shall have eternal life, which gift is the greatest of all the gifts of God" (D&C 14:7). Our investment is obedience, and the return on that investment is eternal life.

When we think about the fluctuations and variables in our economy and the risks we are faced with when we invest our hard-earned money, the Lord's investment plan is incomparable. The only variable is our individual performance, which we alone control. If we come up short, it is because our investment has not been enough to warrant the returns we might have claimed. But each time we choose to improve our efforts—to increase our investments in obedience—the Lord stands ready to fulfill His promise to bless us with spiritual prosperity. Consider the Nephites who, after the Lord's visit to them, lived in perfect obedience for two hundred years. Was their investment worth it? "And surely there could not be a happier people among all the people who had been created by the hand of God" (4 Ne. 1:16). Talk about spiritual prosperity!

> *Eternal life is not for the fainthearted or for those whose faith and performance fluctuate when the going gets tough.*

Eternal life is not for the fainthearted or for those whose faith and performance fluctuate when the going gets tough. The words of an insightful Book of Mormon prophet remind us that we must be humble and obedient to claim the blessings of spiritual prosperity. King Benjamin's list of the qualities that fit us for eternal life include gaining a knowledge of the goodness of God and of His wisdom, patience, and long-suffering; trusting in the Savior's Atonement; being diligent in keeping the commandments; and enduring to the end (see Mosiah 4:6).

"If thou lovest me thou shalt serve me and keep all my commandments" (D&C 42:29).

The Lord Will Comfort Us

And it came to pass that the Lord did visit them with his Spirit, and said unto them: Be comforted. And they were comforted.

ALMA 17:10

The word *comfort* has many meanings and connotations in our lives. We cherish our comfort zones—places or situations that give us a feeling of well-being and safety. We enjoy our comfort foods—foods that are warm and satisfying and agreeable. We appreciate comfort in our physical surroundings—homes that are cozy and well appointed.

But when the physical comforts of the world cannot console us, we yearn for spiritual comfort. It is well for us to know where and to whom we can look for this type of comfort. Nephi knew and recognized that it is the Lord who provides the softening and comforting influence when we are perplexed and troubled: "I did cry unto the Lord; and behold he did visit me, and did soften my heart that I did believe all the words which had been spoken by my father" (1 Ne. 2:16).

The sons of Mosiah felt the Lord's comfort after fasting and praying for the Lord's guidance and protection as they embarked on their mission to the Lamanites. Moroni was comforted by the Lord during his long and lonely wanderings while he was hated and hunted by the Lamanites. In the wretched confines of Liberty Jail, the Lord spoke words of comfort to Joseph Smith, words that never fail to touch and lift our own souls as we read and ponder and internalize them: "My son, peace be unto thy soul; thine adversity and thine afflictions shall be but a small moment; And then, if thou endure it well, God shall exalt thee on high; thou shalt triumph over all thy foes" (D&C 121:7–8).

The Lord spoke tender words of comfort to His confused and bewildered Apostles as they shared the final Feast of the Passover with Him on the eve of His Crucifixion. "I will not leave you comfortless. . . . Peace I leave with you, my peace I give unto you: not as the world giveth, give I unto you. Let not your heart be troubled, neither let it be afraid" (John 14:18, 27).

These words of infinite compassion and comfort are directed at each one of His children. Elder Jeffrey R. Holland tells us that in spite of the Lord's innumerable words of comfort to His children, we as Latter-day Saints

> *Do we have the faith to believe and accept His comfort, His peace, His promise that we do not have to be afraid?*

often resist or fail to understand His promise of peace. Surely it must apply to someone else. He goes on to say that when we fail to let the Savior's love and comfort penetrate our troubled hearts, the Savior is grieved by our lack of confidence in His loving care (see *Trusting Jesus* [Salt Lake City: Deseret Book, 2003], 68).

"Therefore, fear not, little flock. . . . Look unto me in every thought; doubt not, fear not" (D&C 6:34, 36).

❧

"For thou hast been a strength to the poor, a strength to the needy in his distress, a refuge from the storm, a shadow from the heat, when the blast of the terrible ones is as a storm against the wall"
(Isa. 25:4).

To Be Learned Is Good

O that cunning plan of the evil one! O the vainness, and the frailties, and the foolishness of men! When they are learned they think they are wise, and they hearken not unto the counsel of God, for they set it aside, supposing they know of themselves, wherefore, their wisdom is foolishness and it profiteth them not. And they shall perish. But to be learned is good if they hearken unto the counsels of God.

2 Ne. 9:28–29

The Lord has admonished us to be a learned and an educated people, regardless of our chosen vocation or profession. We read in the Doctrine and Covenants: "Seek ye out of the best books words of wisdom; seek learning, even by study and also by faith" (D&C 88:118).

Those who feel we should study only the scriptures miss out on marvelous works of literature, science, and other disciplines. On the other end of the spectrum, those who avidly read everything *except* the scriptures deny themselves the pleasures of the Lord's words of wisdom. In the dedicatory prayer of the Kirtland Temple, the Prophet Joseph Smith reiterated the Lord's counsel regarding learning, emphasizing that there are two crucial elements in the learning process: study and faith (see D&C 109:7).

This scripture from 2 Nephi counsels and cautions us about Satan's plan of pride that would have us believe that once we are "well educated," we could certainly teach the Lord a thing or two. After all, He surely is behind the times when it comes to our sophisticated and technologically advanced society. How ridiculous! Who knows more about everything than the Lord, the Creator of heaven and earth?

Another falsehood of Satan is that once we are learned, we "realize" that the scriptures are second-class, out-of-date, and out-of-fashion. Nephi knew well the dangers of this train of thought when he wrote, "And they shall contend one with another; and they shall teach with their learning, and deny the Holy Ghost, which giveth utterance" (2 Ne. 28:4).

The Savior had bold words for the Pharisees of His time: "Ye are they which justify yourselves before men; but God knoweth your hearts; for that which is highly esteemed among men is abomination in the sight of God" (Luke 16:15). We would all do well to heed this advice.

> *Who knows more about everything than the Lord, the Creator of heaven and earth?*

Consider Sherem and Korihor. Jacob characterizes Sherem as being "learned, that he had a perfect knowledge of the language of the people; wherefore, he could use much flattery, and much power of speech" (Jacob 7:4). And Alma 30:31 tells us that Korihor spoke articulately "in great swelling words." Both were "learned," but refused to hearken to the counsels of God. Indeed, they denied the very Source of all learning.

Coupled with faith in God and our knowledge that He is the source of all light and truth, we should eagerly seek and love learning in all ways that will enlighten us and give us true wisdom.

"A scorner seeketh wisdom, and findeth it not: but knowledge is easy unto him that understandeth" (Prov. 14:6).

THE NATURAL MAN

For the natural man is an enemy to God, and has been from the fall of Adam, and will be, forever and ever, unless he yields to the enticings of the Holy Spirit, and putteth off the natural man and becometh a saint through the atonement of Christ the Lord, and becometh as a child, submissive, meek, humble, patient, full of love, willing to submit to all things which the Lord seeth fit to inflict upon him, even as a child doth submit to his father.

MOSIAH 3:19

The wording of this scripture may at first glance seem a bit harsh and discouraging; however, it is one of the most positive and hopeful messages we find in the Book of Mormon. The Fall of Adam relegated God's children to a temporal world beset with temptations and trials. Separated from the physical presence of God, we are thus subject to the temptations of Satan. If that was the end, we would be truly hopeless.

But our separation from God's presence does not mean that we are left to our own vices and devices. Fortunately, a loving Father foresaw our need for redemption. Therefore, He sent His Beloved Son as a willing sacrifice to atone for our sins so that we would not perish in our natural state, but have the blessings of eternal life in the presence of God and our gracious Redeemer.

Through the gift and power of prayer we can establish a relationship with Deity that guides us in understanding and finding comfort in that greatest of all gifts. The lines of communication with our Heavenly Father are open and free at all times. There will never be a busy signal or a "wrong number" or a "temporarily out of order" message. The brother of Jared knew this to be true when he said, "O Lord, thou hast given us a commandment that we must call upon thee" (Ether 3:2).

The Savior teaches us that putting off the natural man means becoming as little children, pure and pleasing in God's sight—deserving of the blessings of the Atonement. "Therefore, whoso repenteth and cometh unto me as a little child, him will I receive, for of such is the kingdom of

> *Our separation from God's presence does not mean that we are left to our own vices and devices.*

God. Behold, for such I have laid down my life, and have taken it up again; therefore repent, and come unto me ye ends of the earth, and be saved" (3 Ne. 9:22).

The message of the gospel is one of hope and encouragement. We have the opportunity to resist our natural inclinations and weaknesses and, through the Atonement of Jesus Christ, use our free agency to change and become changed from a natural to a spiritual state.

> *"It matters not what may befall,*
> *What threat'ning hand hangs over me;*
> *He is my rampart through it all,*
> *My refuge from mine enemy"* (Hymns, *no. 114*).

ACHIEVING PERFECTION

Therefore I would that ye should be perfect even as I, or your Father who is in heaven is perfect.

3 NE. 12:48

So many of our tasks and responsibilities have deadlines, and missing them can result in negative consequences and penalties. It is well to note that the admonition to be perfect does not have a deadline attached to it that, if missed, means we have failed and there are no second chances. The Lord in His infinite love and mercy knows that our goal of perfection is achieved one obedient step at a time. Just like any other work of art, we do not become whole or finished or fully developed without much polishing, touching up, and even starting over.

Our progress toward perfection is incremental, dependent on our gradual but steady efforts to better ourselves, as did the people in the city of Enoch. This was also the case with the Savior, who "received not of the fulness at first, but continued from grace to grace, until he received a fulness" (D&C 93:13).

For those of us who have ever worked on a jigsaw puzzle that has hundreds or even thousands of pieces, we know that it takes patience—and that it is put together one small section at a time until eventually all the sections are finished and we have a finished product that matches the picture on the box. The Savior knows how our finished picture should look, and He is patient and helpful in guiding us through each section, cheering us on and telling us to never give up until we have achieved a pleasing wholeness.

There may be times when we look at someone else's puzzle and see what we perceive as their tactical errors or their lack of perceptible progress; then we feel better about our own plodding efforts. This mindset merely distracts us and tempts us onto paths of rationalization and procrastination. Integral to becoming perfect like our Savior is the ability and desire to lift and bless and help others along the way, just as the Savior lifts and blesses us.

As we progress toward perfection, small successes build toward the desired and ultimate outcome. Ralph Waldo Emerson penned these words that remind us of the relevance of our efforts:

"Success is:
To laugh often and much;
To win the respect of intelligent people and the affection of children;
To earn the appreciation of honest critics and endure the betrayal of false friends;

> *The Lord in His infinite love and mercy knows that our goal of perfection is achieved one obedient step at a time.*

To appreciate beauty, to find the best in others;
To leave the world a bit better, whether by a healthy child, a garden patch, or a redeemed social condition;
To know even one life has breathed easier because you have lived.
This is to have succeeded."

*More purity give me, More strength to o'er come,
More freedom from earth stains, More longing for home.
More fit for the kingdom, More used would I be,
More blessed and holy—More, Savior, like thee"* (Hymns, no. 131).

FILLED WITH THE FRUIT OF THE GOSPEL

And because of your diligence and your faith and your patience with the word in nourishing it, that it may take root in you, behold, by and by ye shall pluck the fruit thereof, which is most precious, which is sweet above all that is sweet, and which is white above all that is white, yea, and pure above all that is pure; and ye shall feast upon this fruit even until ye are filled, that ye hunger not, neither shall ye thirst. Then, my brethren, ye shall reap the rewards of your faith, and your diligence, and patience, and long-suffering, waiting for the tree to bring forth fruit unto you.

ALMA 32:42–43

Springtime is a season of hope and renewal. We joyfully watch for signs of new life in nature; we anticipate the sun's warming rays and eagerly look forward to planting seeds that will result in a beautiful harvest. We turn the soil and make sure that it is fertile and ready for the seeds; once we plant the seeds, we must be diligent in providing them with water and proper nutrients to ensure their growth. Once they begin to grow and flourish, we must then make sure that weeds do not overrun the tender sprouts. After all this, we have every reason to hope that our diligence and patience will produce the desired results.

And so it is with the word of God in our lives. Alma wisely chose a metaphor to which we can all relate when he explains that our diligence and faith and patience are the "nutrients" that ensure that the gospel will take root in our lives. Strong roots produce strong plants and good fruit.

Alma speaks of a fruit that is precious and sweet and pure and white—the gospel of Jesus Christ. It is the same fruit that Lehi and Nephi saw in vision; it was "most sweet," with a whiteness to exceed all whiteness, and "desirable above all other fruit" (see 1 Ne. 8:10–12). We all have our favorite fruit and we eagerly anticipate enjoying its abundance when the season is right, hoping that the crop will be sweet and satisfying. We are saddened when the season for that fruit is past, or when it was not a good year and the fruit was not quite as sweet and satisfying as we had hoped. We long for a time when we will again be able to enjoy that special treat in its peak of goodness.

The fruit Alma speaks of is always in season, and the quality is consistent. There are

> *The gospel of Jesus Christ is pure, and it fills and completely satisfies our spirits.*

no disappointing crops or harvests, nor do we ever feel empty or hungry once we have partaken of it. The gospel of Jesus Christ is pure, and it fills and completely satisfies our spirits.

The Lord promises us that as we faithfully and patiently and diligently nourish the fruit of the gospel in our lives, the fruit will be consistently sweet and abundant. "He that is faithful, the same shall be kept and blessed with much fruit" (D&C 52:34).

> *"And now, my brethren, I desire that ye shall plant this word in your hearts, and as it beginneth to swell even so nourish it by your faith. And behold, it will become a tree, springing up in you unto everlasting life" (Alma 33:23).*

EAT, DRINK, AND BE MERRY

Yea, and there shall be many which shall say: Eat, drink, and be merry, for tomorrow we die; and it shall be well with us. And there shall also be many which shall say: Eat, drink, and be merry; nevertheless, fear God—he will justify in committing a little sin; yea, lie a little, take the advantage of one because of his words, dig a pit for thy neighbor; there is no harm in this; and do all these things, for tomorrow we die; and if it so be that we are guilty, God will beat us with a few stripes, and at last we shall be saved in the kingdom of God.

2 NE. 28:7–8

Throughout the Book of Mormon, we see numerous examples of people who bought into the very philosophy of which Nephi speaks—a philosophy authored by Lucifer, the father of all lies. It is based on the supposition that we can be content with momentary gratifications, ignoring and denying any significant eternal consequences.

The prophet Mormon prophesied that the Book of Mormon would come forth in a time of great wickedness—in a world beset with sin, corruption, spiritual pollution, and "all manner of abominations" (Morm. 8:31). He foresaw that it would be a time when people would be hedonistic, self-serving, and self-deceiving, denying the very Atonement of Jesus Christ by their smug claims of immunity from personal responsibility for any wrongdoing. It does not take any stretch of our imagination to see that Mormon was talking about our time.

We are horrified by blatant examples of such behavior, but

there are less visible and more subtle manifestations of the "eat, drink, and be merry" train of thought. It moves quickly, quietly, and efficiently, programmed for few (if any) stops along the way. Once onboard, it is easy to relax and enjoy the ride and just "go with the flow." Clever and colorful advertisements posted on its walls lull and comfort us:

"Telling a few small lies is relatively harmless." "Taking advantage of a few shady schemes for financial gain is okay; after all, everyone is doing it." "Letting someone else take the blame for our wrongdoing can save us a lot of personal embarrassment." "Twisting someone's words to put them in a bad light can often make us look a little better than we really are." "Putting minimal effort into our callings and skimping a bit on our tithes and offerings saves us a bunch of time and money."

And what is the ultimate destination of that train?

> *Let us avoid Satan's deceitful and subtle flattery while seeking instead the Lord's forthright direction and approbation.*

Well, the conductor is intent on driving it "carefully down to hell," where passengers will be unceremoniously tossed out without so much as a backward glance.

Let us avoid Satan's deceitful and subtle flattery while seeking instead the Lord's forthright direction and approbation. It is imperative that we board the right train, whose ultimate destination is the kingdom of God.

⌁

"Look unto me in every thought; doubt not, fear not. . . . be faithful, keep my commandments, and ye shall inherit the kingdom of heaven" (D&C 6:36–37).

FAITH

And now as I said concerning faith—faith is not to have a perfect knowledge of things; therefore if ye have faith ye hope for things which are not seen, which are true.

ALMA 32:21

We believe that the first principle of the gospel is faith in the Lord Jesus Christ. It is the undergirding principle upon which all gospel growth is built. *Hoping for things not seen* defines faith perfectly. We are all familiar with the saying "Seeing is believing," but when applied to the principle of faith, it really is better expressed the other way around: "Believing is seeing."

Consider the following examples of those who had not seen, but yet believed. In each instance, faith precedes the miracle—"For if there be no faith among the children of men God can do no miracle among them; wherefore, he showed not himself until after their faith" (Ether 12:12).

By faith, Noah built an ark when the sun was shining and there was not a rain cloud in the sky; by faith, cripples and lepers were healed, and the blind were made to see. By faith, the waters of the Red Sea were parted and the children of Israel escaped the oncoming Egyptian hordes; by faith, Abraham obediently laid his only son on a sacrificial altar. By faith, the brother of Jared saw the finger of the Lord and subsequently saw the Lord Himself; by faith, Nephi built a ship that sailed safely across a vast ocean to a new and unknown land. By faith, Alma took a band of believers into the wilderness to escape the wrath of a wicked king; by faith, the lives of the stripling warriors were preserved as they fought in defense of their freedom.

By faith, a young Joseph Smith saw and heard God the Father and Jesus Christ; by faith, Saints traversed a vast frontier to find their promised land. By faith, temples fill the earth, and Saints of countless nations are blessed.

Each of these examples demonstrates faith—not in the arm of flesh, or in destinations, or in man-made plans, or in structures—but faith in the Lord Jesus Christ. They exemplify what Moroni said regarding faith: "Faith is things which are hoped for and not seen; wherefore, dispute not because ye see not, for ye receive no witness until after the trial of your faith" (Ether 12:6).

> *Hoping for things not seen defines faith perfectly.*

The Prophet Joseph Smith teaches us that faith is a great gift, and is a prerequisite to receiving all of God's other gifts (*Teachings of the Prophet Joseph Smith*, comp. Joseph Fielding Smith [Salt Lake City: Deseret Book, 1976], 270). He further states that "Faith comes by hearing the word of God through the testimony of the servants of God; that testimony is always attended by the spirit of prophecy and revelation" (*Teachings*, 145).

❧

"Behold, verily, verily, I say unto you, this is my gospel; and remember that they shall have faith in me or they can in nowise be saved" (D&C 33:12).

The Light and Life of the World

He is the light and the life of the world; yea, a light that is endless, that can never be darkened; yea, and also a life which is endless, that there can be no more death.

MOSIAH 16:9

There is nothing more frustrating than a dim or burned-out light. We live by light, and we crave its illumination for reading, for handiwork, for hobbies, for housework—for just about everything we want to accomplish. Wouldn't it be grand if someone invented light bulbs that would truly live up to all the promises of longevity and performance?

Our spirits crave illumination just as do as our physical counterparts. Fortunately, when it comes to the spiritual scenario, there is a Light that is guaranteed never to wear out or vary in quality. The scriptures are full and brimming over with this promise. And where do we find that miraculous light? It is, of course, in the Savior. His Light can "never be darkened"; it is "endless"; it is the "city that is set on a hill" (Matt. 5:14); it is the Light of the sun, moon, and stars combined; it is the Light by which everything was created; it is the "light which is in all things, which is the law by which all things are governed, even the power of God who sitteth upon his throne, who is in the bosom of eternity, who is in the midst of all things" (D&C 88:13).

The only chance of a power outage is if we choose to reject or shut out His Light, and even in that event, His Light is simply rejected but never extinguished. Like small children who put their hands over their eyes and then suppose that we can no longer see them, we too can close our spiritual eyes. Nevertheless, the Lord's

Light is still shining, awaiting the moment when we "open our eyes," step out of the darkness, and let it illuminate our lives.

The Savior is also the life of the world. His Resurrection makes this so and carries the same guarantee as His Light—**it works for everyone all the time.** "For as in Adam all men die, even so in Christ shall *all* be made alive" (1 Cor. 15:22; emphasis added). There are, however, two aspects to His declaration that He is the life of the world. Not only does He promise a restoration of our physical bodies after death, but His Atonement gives us the hope of eternal life, or life in His presence. The full blessings of the Atonement, however, are conditional upon our willingness to repent.

> *Fortunately, when it comes to the spiritual scenario, there is a Light that is guaranteed never to wear out.*

He is anxious for us all to receive this fulness of life. He is come "that [we] might have life, and that [we] might have it more abundantly" (John 10:10). In pondering the wondrous blessings of His Light and Life, we find wisdom in these words:

The Lord is my light, my all and in all.
There is in his sight no darkness at all.
He is my Redeemer, my Savior and King.
With Saints and with angels his praises I'll sing (*Hymns*, no. 89).

"O house of Jacob, come ye, and let us walk in the light of the Lord"
(Isa: 2:5).

LOYALTY

And it came to pass that he rent his coat; and he took a piece thereof, and wrote upon it—In memory of our God, our religion, and freedom, and our peace, our wives, and our children—and he fastened it upon the end of a pole.

ALMA 46:12

Loyalty is a quality to be admired and acquired. In this scripture, Moroni reminds us of the priority of our loyalties. While Moroni does not specifically mention the word *loyalty* in this scripture, the word *memory* is so closely related as to be interchangeable. Moroni could have just as easily said, "In loyalty to. . . ."

Each week as we partake of the sacrament, we promise to remember our Savior in order to better keep His commandments. His first and great commandment is to "love the Lord thy God with all thy heart, and with all thy soul, and with all thy mind" (Matt. 22:37). This demands the utmost loyalty and remembrance, but we can love and remember only someone we truly know.

The second commandment is to "love thy neighbor as thyself" (Matt. 22:38), and this begins at home. Where better to keep this commandment than within our own families—in our relationships with our spouses, our children, and our siblings? Do we remember to honor our promises to love and care for one another? To always conduct ourselves in a way that we would be pleased to have our families remember?

Moroni's banner also exhorts us to remember our religion. We might ask ourselves how we could ever forget that, but think about the awful examples of those who *forgot* their religion. The very people who had prompted Moroni's call to loyalty were once-loyal members of the Church who had fallen into such a disgraceful state of apostasy that their only intent was to massacre with barbarous cruelty "those who were once their brethren" (Alma 48:24).

Think what a stirring experience it must have been to see Moroni going forth among the people, "waving the rent part of his garment in the air, that all might see the writing which he had written upon the rent part" (Alma 46:19). With such a visible reminder, wouldn't it have been easier for Moroni's people to "remember" than it is for us? Surely such a righteous rally would keep our loyalties uppermost in our minds, jog our memories more dramatically. Yet, we have this same "title of liberty" written in our hearts through our baptismal and sacrament covenants. It is that same spiritual contract, and it warrants close and frequent scrutiny.

> *We have this same "title of liberty" written in our hearts through our baptismal and sacrament covenants.*

"*Up, awake ye defenders of Zion!*
The foe's at the door of your homes;
Let each heart be the heart of a lion,
Unyielding and proud as he roams.
Remember the trials of Missouri;
Forget not the courage of Nauvoo.
When the enemy host is before you,
Stand firm and be faithful and true" (Hymns, no. 248).

Steadfastness, Selflessness, and Obedience

Blessed art thou, Nephi, for those things which thou hast done; for I have beheld how thou has with unwearyingness declared the word, which I have given unto thee, unto this people. And thou hast not feared them, and hast not sought thine own life, but hast sought my will, and to keep my commandments.

HEL. 10:4

In this loving compliment and tribute from the Lord to one of His beloved prophets, we are reminded of those qualities the Lord esteems in His children: steadfastness, selflessness, and obedience.

The Lord respects and honors steadfastness in those who choose to serve and follow Him. This implies strength and dedication despite all odds. The prophet Nephi, to whom these words were spoken, truly exemplified this trait; he was scorned and conspired against and threatened in various ways and on many occasions. It would have been easy and even defensible for him to have used such familiar phrases as "How many times have I told you?" or "I'm not going to tell you again." Yet it never occurred to him to cease to teach his people the word of God, even when it continued to fall on deaf ears.

Prophets and leaders in all dispensations have possessed this same dedication, and faithful members of the Church throughout the world demonstrate their "unwearyingness" as they serve faithfully in whatever callings they are given, despite challenges and setbacks.

The words of the Savior teach us the essence of selflessness: "Therefore take no thought, saying, What shall we eat? or, What shall we drink? or, Wherewithal shall we be clothed? For your heavenly Father knoweth that ye have need of all these things. But seek ye first the kingdom of God and his righteousness, and all these things shall be added unto you" (3 Ne. 13:31–33).

The Savior promises us that if we seek first "the kingdom of God, and his righteousness," then "all these things shall be added unto [us]" (Matt. 6:33). It all comes down to our priorities and our willingness to lose ourselves in service to others, to focus outward rather than inward.

The Lord wants us to do His will—to be obedient—and has set the perfect example. He never asks us to do any-thing that He has not done:

> *We are reminded of those qualities the Lord esteems in His children: steadfast-ness, selflessness, and obedience.*

"And behold, I am the light and the life of the world; and I have drunk out of that bitter cup which the Father hath given me, and have glori-fied the Father in taking upon me the sins of the world, in the which I have suffered the will of the Father in *all* things from the beginning" (3 Ne. 11:11; emphasis added). Each small act of obe-dience is rewarded with an outpouring of God's blessings and ap-proval. As we do His will, it will also be our privilege to hear His words of approval: "Blessed art thou" (Luke 1:42); "Well done, thou good and faithful servant" (Matt. 25:21); "Be of good cheer" (Mark 6:50); and "Lift up your head" (3 Ne. 1:13). His blessings will be abundant in our lives.

᷍

"Behold, this is your work, to keep my commandments, yea, with all your might, mind and strength" (D&C 11:20).

PRIDE OF THE WORLD 80

And it came to pass that I saw and bear record, that the great and spacious building was the pride of the world; and it fell, and the fall thereof was exceedingly great.

1 NE. 11:36

Both Lehi and Nephi saw a marvelous vision in which there was a large and spacious building that represented the pride of the world. The building was filled to overflowing with people of all ages who scorned and mocked those who were endeavoring to stay the course and live by the word of God. The building's position is significant: "It stood as it were in the air, high above the earth" (1 Ne. 8:26), so that those who were crowded into its portals were looking down, all the better to point their fingers at those who were struggling through mists and murky waters. This is characteristic of pride; it is always looking in any other direction rather than up to God.

When pride looks inward, love of self is one of its best accomplishments. Where there is pride there is no room for love of anyone else, including God. Paul characterized it as a loss of natural affection (see 2 Tim. 3:2).

When pride looks sideways, it spawns contention and competition; however, it always demands to be the winner. There is no room for anyone else's accomplishments. When it puts its arms around someone else, it is usually the gesture that precedes the push that will take them out of the running for the spotlight. Its disdainful glance is filled with envy and denies the equality of brotherhood. It cannot bear the thought that someone might have something it doesn't have, nor can it bear the thought of sharing any of its "belongings." C. S. Lewis said: "Pride gets no pleasure out of having something, only out of having more of it than the next man. . . . It is the comparison that makes you proud: the pleasure of being above the rest. Once the element of competition has gone, pride has gone" (*Mere Christianity* [New York: Macmillan, 1952], 109–10).

When pride looks downward, its arrogant stare warns that its learning and wisdom exceed that of all others. There is nothing worth learning that it doesn't already know.

Pride leaves a path of destruction of sacred and precious things in its wake. In his

> *Where there is pride there is no room for love of anyone else, including God.*

legendary sermon on pride, President Ezra Taft Benson reminds members of the Church that the Book of Mormon is a classic example of how a nation can fall because of pride. He also calls our attention to a bold reminder from the Lord, issued in these latter days: "And if ye seek the riches which it is the will of the Father to give unto you, ye shall be the richest of all people, for ye shall have the riches of eternity; and it must needs be that the riches of the earth are mine to give; but beware of pride, lest ye become as the Nephites of old" (D&C 38:39) (see "Beware of Pride," *Ensign*, May 1989).

"Pride goeth before destruction, and an haughty spirit before a fall" (Prov. 16:18).

Learn in Thy Youth

O, remember, my son, and learn wisdom in thy youth; yea, learn in thy youth to keep the commandments of God.

Alma 37:35

It is interesting how often the word *remember* appears in the scriptures. It is a sacred admonition used often by the Lord and His prophets to give us a spiritual nudge. When we get together to visit with family or friends, the greater part of our conversations often revolve around the words, *Remember when.* . . . We happily reminisce and enjoy our encounters in memory's corridors. It is the same when we examine our tender memories of loved ones who have passed beyond the veil; we would never forget them, nor would we want them to forget us.

And so it is with things pertaining to our spiritual relationships. Alma's admonition to his son echoes the Savior's invitation to all His children. It is an earnest plea to which all parents can relate. Once our children learn how to walk, talk, dress, and feed themselves, they never forget these basic skills that are stepping stones to more difficult and sophisticated accomplishments. Basic gospel principles and behaviors taught and learned early are likewise the foundation upon which future decisions, growth, and wisdom depend. Sometimes there is a spiritual memory lapse, but if those teachings are in place and have been an integral part of our children's lives from an early age, they can be recalled—and those reminiscences will be a positive call to action: "Train up a child in the way he should go: and when he is old, he will not depart from it" (Prov. 22:6).

Spiritual memories can be awakened by memories of lessons learned in loving homes, taught by loving parents and reinforced by a loving heavenly Parent. We are commanded to "bring up [our] children in light and truth" (D&C 93:40), and if we do that, the quiet promptings of the Holy Ghost will remind them that they are in-deed children of God who need to "be about their Father's business" (see Luke 2:49).

> *Spiritual memories can be awakened by memories of lessons learned in loving homes, taught by loving parents.*

Our children will not remember what they have not been taught, and we as parents are clearly instructed to teach them "the doctrine of repentance, faith in Christ the Son of the living God, and of baptism and the gift of the Holy Ghost . . . and to pray, and to walk uprightly before the Lord" (D&C 68:25, 28). With these teachings clearly in place, spiritual memories can be stored and stirred. Sometimes we may need to wait patiently for that day when *Remember when* assumes an eternal significance in our children's lives, but it will be a joyful family reunion for both earthly and heavenly parents.

❧

"For thou art my hope, O Lord God: thou art my trust from my youth" (Ps. 71:5).

Pleasant **82** Message of Peace

And it came to pass that there came a voice unto them, yea, a pleasant voice, as if it were a whisper, saying: Peace, peace be unto you, because of your faith in my Well Beloved, who was from the foundation of the world.

Hel. 5:47

Within the dark and confining walls of a prison, among the most vile of sinners whose taunting and loud voices were most likely reminding them of their impending executions, Nephi and Lehi, the missionary sons of Helaman, had a most amazing experience. As they were about to be slain, these two emissaries of God were encircled about with a pillar of fire, and the thick walls of the prison shook as if they were about to fall. However, something even more significant was about to happen.

As an understandably "awful fear" and darkness came upon the much-subdued prisoners, they heard a voice that immediately captured their attention—not because it was loud and ear-splitting, but because "it was a still voice of perfect mildness, as if it had been a whisper, and it did pierce even to the very soul" (Hel. 5:30).

A quiet voice is the most dramatic and effective way to get anyone's attention and to prepare them for a message of great importance. In all instances, the message of the mild voice is the same—it is the message of repentance and faith in the Lord Jesus Christ. From this scripture we learn that to those who are humble and willing to listen, the voice of the Messenger is also a pleasing voice, gratifying and satisfying in its message. Hearts are softened, and misguided lives are changed. "I will hear what

God the Lord will speak: for he will speak peace unto his people, and to his saints" (Ps. 85:8).

Jacob refers to the message as "the pleasing word of God, yea, the word which healeth the wounded soul" (Jacob 2:8), souls that are wounded by sin and sorrow and disappointment and loss. It is a message that carries with it a promise of peace that can be matched by no other source. "And the peace of God, which passeth all understanding, shall keep your hearts and minds through Jesus Christ" (Philip. 4:7). When the tempest raged over the Sea of Galilee, the Savior did not shout to be heard above the wind and the storm. He simply and quietly said, "Peace, be still. And the wind ceased, and there was a great calm" (Mark 4:39). His voice and His message can likewise

> *A quiet voice is the most effective way to get anyone's attention and to prepare them for a message of great importance.*

calm all the storms that rage in our lives. In a movingly beautiful passage of scripture, the prophet Abinadi tells us, quoting the prophet Isaiah, "For O how beautiful upon the mountains are the feet of him that bringeth good tidings, that is the founder of peace, yea, even the Lord, who has redeemed his people; yea, him who has granted salvation unto his people" (Mosiah 15:18). Surely the promise of salvation can speak nothing but peace and healing to our souls.

❧

"The Lord bless thee, and keep thee: The Lord make his face shine upon thee, and be gracious unto thee: The Lord lift up his countenance upon thee, and give thee peace" (Num. 6:24–26).

Now Is the Time

For behold, this life is the time for men to prepare to meet God; yea, behold the day of this life is the day for men to perform their labors.

ALMA 34:32

We are all familiar with the saying, "There's no time like the present"—a saying that applies in very *real* ways and in *many* ways, both physical and spiritual. Students who study diligently and consistently can expect to do well on a final exam. Conversely, those who count on an eleventh-hour cramming session can usually expect a failing grade. We are constantly being reminded to have adequate supplies on hand for times of need that may be occasioned by natural disasters, illness, unemployment, or other unexpected emergencies. When the need arises, it is too late to heed that reminder; the time for preparation has passed.

That same philosophy governs our spiritual preparations. The Savior illustrated this in the parable of the ten virgins who had been invited to a wedding celebration. Five were adequately prepared for any contingency, carrying along some extra oil—just in case—while the other five figured that what was in their lamps should do the job quite nicely. When it became evident that the guest of honor was going to be later arriving than expected, the provident virgins wisely refused to share any of their oil—just in case. While the improvident virgins ran out to find an oil merchant, the party started behind closed doors without them. And once the doors were closed, there was no admittance. In relating this parable, the Savior was speaking to members of the Church, not to the world at large, sadly anticipating that a large percentage of us will miss the "party" due to a lack of poor or delayed spiritual preparation.

We make our spiritual preparations in anticipation of the time when we will meet the Savior, either at our going or His Coming. In either event, we have no way of knowing just when that will happen, so there can be no last-minute scrambling to replenish our spiritual pantries and no cramming for "finals." The Lord tells us that "If [we] are prepared [we] shall not fear" (D&C 38:30)—a simple formula that never fails.

> *We prepare in anticipation of the time when we will meet the Savior, either at our going or His coming.*

The scriptures refer to our time of preparation as a probationary state, a trial period in which the mettle of our obedience is tested: "Therefore this life became a probationary state; a time to prepare to meet God; a time to prepare for that endless state which has been spoken of by us, which is after the resurrection of the dead" (Alma 12:24). *Endless* is a long time in which to find ourselves in the wrong state, but just right if we are where we really want to be—and where the Lord wants us to be.

❧

"*Improve the shining moments; don't let them pass you by.
Work while the sun is radiant; work for the night draws nigh.
We cannot bid the sunbeams to lengthen out their stay,
Nor can we ask the shadows to ever stay away*" (Hymns, no. 226).

AVERSION TO SIN

O Lord, wilt thou redeem my soul? Wilt thou deliver me out of the hands of mine enemies? Wilt thou make me that I may shake at the appearance of sin?

2 Ne. 2:31

When we think of the prophet Nephi, we usually do not tend to think of someone who was troubled by a long list of sins, but rather as someone overwhelmed by a long list of sinners. Yet his candor in his eloquent psalm reminds us that he was very human, with shortcomings that sent him to the Lord on his knees in a heartfelt plea for divine assistance in overcoming those things in which he felt he might have fallen short. His request for the wisdom and insight to recognize and rebuff sin in any of its many forms is a good indication of the strength of this great prophet's spiritual integrity.

The idea of shaking *at* the appearance of sin is very different than the idea of shaking *after* we have committed a sin. Our instinctive reaction to something repulsive or frightening is to turn away and run as fast as possible in the other direction; however, the least hesitation on our part can slow that run to a jog, then to a walk, and then to a standstill that gradually becomes a pivotal turn toward the very thing we had once found so abhorrent. Alexander Pope penned these succinct words that capture the essence of this incremental acceptance:

> Vice is a monster of so frightful mien,
> As to be hated, needs but to be seen;
> Yet seen too oft, familiar with her face,
> We first endure, then pity, then embrace.

We should never say how much the devil tempts us, but only how strongly we are inclined toward rather than repulsed by his suggestions. Shaking at the appearance of sin may mean coordinating our deed with our creed, making up our minds firmly about what we truly believe and what we truly embrace. Do we believe in being *sort of* honest, true, chaste, and benevolent? In *sometimes* seeking after that which is praiseworthy and lovely and of good report? Or are we as committed as Nephi in our desire to give sin the cold shoulder?

We know that only our perfect Elder Brother—He and He alone—could experience in the Garden of Gethsemane all our sorrow for all our sins. As the sinless Lamb of God, only Jesus could perform this great act of grace in our behalf for all the sins that we would not shun. Unlike the rest of us, He "cannot look upon sin with the least degree of allowance" (D&C 1:31).

> *Shaking at the appearance of sin may mean making up our minds firmly about what we truly embrace.*

The Lord's suffering in the Garden of Gethsemane constituted the most infinite and intense example of shaking at the appearance of sin—the collective sins of all mankind. Only His unconditional love for us and His desire to do His Father's will made it possible for Him to see it through to the end. The evidence of our gratitude and our love for Him lies in the degree to which we are willing to give sin a wide berth.

"Abhor that which is evil; cleave to that which is good"
(Rom. 12:9).

PURE IN HEART

But behold, I, Jacob, would speak unto you that are pure in heart. Look unto God with firmness of mind, and pray unto him with exceeding faith, and he will console you in your afflictions, and he will plead your cause, and send down justice upon those who seek your destruction.

JACOB 3:1

Jacob directs his message of hope and comfort to those who are pure in heart. We know that the Lord is not concerned with our outward appearance; He uses the heart as the measure of our true character and as the criteria by which He will judge us. "For the Lord seeth not as man seeth; for man looketh on the outward appearance, but the Lord looketh on the heart" (1 Sam. 16:7).

Jacob reminds us that those who are pure in heart have some very good habits, one of which is being firm in our commitment to and trust in God. This means, of course, that we are steady and immovable in that trust and commitment, even when the going gets tough. The pure in heart have also developed a habit of faithful and diligent prayer. Again, this means that our prayers are not just cries for help when we are troubled and distressed; rather, they are an open and ongoing line of communication with our Heavenly Father, who desires to hear from us at all times and in all the "seasons" of our lives.

In the Sermon on the Mount, the Savior tells us: "Blessed are *all* the pure in heart, for they shall see God" (3 Ne. 12:8; emphasis added). We stand in reverent awe when we read scriptural accounts of those who have literally seen God. Moses saw Him face to face and talked with Him (see Moses 1:2); the brother of Jared was privileged to see Him (see Ether 3:13); King Lamoni saw his Redeemer (see Alma 19:13); and in our own dispensation, the Prophet Joseph Smith saw Him (see JS—H 1:17; D&C 76:23).

The majority of us will probably not have these kinds of personal and literal encounters. But we see Him as He works His wonders in our lives. We see Him as He consoles and comforts us. He comes to us in so many ways—through the words of the scriptures; through the words of our modern-day prophets; through the kind charity of others, and through the ministrations of the Holy Ghost. He pleads for us; He is our advocate with Heavenly Father, our merciful Redeemer whose love and encouragement continually purifies our hearts. He is our Elder Brother who stands ready to defend and protect us when others would seek to harm us. "I will fear no evil: for thou art with me; thy rod and thy staff they comfort me" (Ps. 23:4).

> *"For the Lord seeth not as man seeth; for man looketh on the outward appearance, but the Lord looketh on the heart."*

As we become ever more pure in heart, we will continue to see God's hand in our lives, enriching us in countless ways until that time when, through His grace, we receive the ultimate and eternal blessing of seeing Him face to face.

"If with all your hearts ye truly seek me,
Ye shall ever surely find me,
Thus saith our God" (CSB, 15).

SHARING THE SWEETNESS OF THE GOSPEL

And as I partook of the fruit thereof it filled my soul with exceedingly great joy; wherefore, I began to be desirous that my family should partake of it also; for I knew that it was desirable above all other fruit.

1 NE. 8:12

Both Lehi and Nephi were privileged to see the vision of the tree of life, and in that vision they beheld a tree whose fruit they described as being most sweet, exceedingly white, desirable, precious, and joyous to the soul. How did they know so much about this fruit? The answer is quite simple; they tasted it, and they didn't have to be asked twice or coaxed. Their first reactions were those of pure joy, followed immediately by a desire to have their other family members taste the fruit as well. This is an instinct we can easily relate to—when we experience something that enriches us or makes us happy, we want to share that good fortune or happiness with others, particularly members of our own family.

We see this same phenomenon repeated when Enos experienced the sweet comfort of the Lord's forgiveness and gained an understanding of the Atonement of Jesus Christ. He immediately desired the same blessing for his brethren. Alma also felt this generosity of spirit after experiencing redeeming love and forgiveness from the Savior: "Yea, and from that time even until now, I have labored without ceasing, that I might bring souls unto repentance; that I might bring them to taste of the exceeding joy of which I did taste; that they might also be born of God, and be filled with the Holy Ghost" (Alma 36:24).

The tree and its fruit represent the love of God, and because of God's love for us we have the promise of eternal life, which is made possible only through the Atonement of His Only Begotten Son. We want our loved ones to enjoy the blessings of the gospel and feel the love of the Savior and partake of the sweet fruits of His Atonement.

Sometimes we are disappointed when those we love are hesitant to taste the fruit, and our disappointment deepens when they taste the fruit and then decide they don't really like it. It's similar to preparing a delicious meal only to find that someone doesn't really like it or won't even give it the taste test. We tend to take their hesitation or rejection per-

> *We wisely cherish that which is precious, and share it freely and unceasingly with those we love.*

sonally, but, like wise parents in all generations, we follow the example of the Savior and never give up in our efforts to share the sweet fruits of the gospel. Only time will tell when they will take that first taste, or suddenly remember that they like that "flavor" after all.

Nephi testifies that the "fruit is most precious and most desirable above all other fruits; yea, and it is the greatest of all the gifts of God" (1 Ne. 15:36). We wisely cherish that which is precious, and share it freely and unceasingly with those we love.

"For the Lord Jehovah is my strength and my song; he also is become my salvation. Therefore with joy shall ye draw water out of the wells of salvation" (Isa. 12:2–3).

THE 87 ATONEMENT

Wherefore, may God raise you from death by the power of the resurrection, and also from everlasting death by the power of the atonement, that ye may be received into the eternal kingdom of God, that ye may praise him through grace divine. Amen.

2 NE. 10:25

In a powerful discourse, Jacob expounds on the Atonement of Jesus Christ. He explains both the physical and spiritual deaths, reminding us that because of the Fall of Adam, we will all die and experience a separation of body and spirit; the Fall also occasioned a spiritual death, which is a separation from God's presence. Through the Atonement, we will all be resurrected, receiving the restoration of the body and the spirit. The Atonement also provides a restoration of another kind. We will be restored to God's presence to receive His judgments; however, not all of us will be privileged to remain in His presence. That will depend entirely on how well we keep His commandments during our mortal probation.

Christ is the centerpiece of the Church, and as such, it is imperative that we continually seek to enhance our understanding of the Atonement that He wrought in our behalf. The overall purpose of the Atonement is to enable us to return to the presence of God with the potential to become like Him. It is the means by which we can overcome physical death; it is the means through which we overcome the second, or spiritual, death.

The Savior's suffering in Gethsemane provided us with the opportunity to repent and through His grace receive the blessings of eternal life; His suffering on the cross provided us with the gift of restoration of both spirit and body after we die. The alternative is unthinkable. As Jacob tells us, we would be subject to what he refers to as that monster, death and hell—subject to the eternal torments and buffetings of Satan.

The Atonement is a perfect blend of justice, love, and mercy. The words of Isaiah remind us of the completeness of the Atonement and our total reliance on the Savior's grace: "Surely he hath borne our griefs, and carried our sorrows: yet we did esteem him stricken, smitten of God, and afflicted. But he was wounded for our transgressions, he was bruised for our iniquities: the chastisement of our peace was upon him; and

> *Christ is the centerpiece of the Church, so we must continually seek to enhance our understanding of the Atonement.*

with his stripes we are healed" (Isa. 53:4–5). There is no mistaking the powerful message therein. He not only took upon Himself our sins, but all our sorrows, illnesses, griefs, and disappointments. The Savior did it *all* for *all* of us. It is ultimately through His grace that we are saved.

"[It] appears that the great and glorious plan of His redemption was previously provided: the sacrifice prepared: the atonement wrought out in the mind and purpose of God, even in the person of the Son, through whom man was now to look for acceptance and through whose merits he was now taught that he alone could find redemption" (Teachings of the Prophet Joseph Smith, *comp. Joseph Fielding Smith [Salt Lake City: Deseret Book, 1976], 57–58).

TRIED AND TRUE

But, behold, the righteous, the saints of the Holy One of Israel, they who have believed in the Holy One of Israel, they who have endured the crosses of the world, and despised the shame of it, they shall inherit the kingdom of God, which was prepared for them from the foundation of the world, and their joy shall be full forever.

2 NE. 9:18

The fifth principle of the gospel is enduring to the end. We often hear that the word *well* should be added so that it says "enduring *well* to the end." In fact, the Savior said this very thing to Joseph Smith when he cried out from the confines of Liberty Jail. The Lord promised Joseph that his trials would constitute but a small moment in the eternal scheme of things, and that if he endured them well, "God shall exalt thee on high; thou shalt triumph over all thy foes" (D&C 121:8).

The key to appreciating this advice is to keep an eternal perspective. Did Joseph triumph over all his earthly foes? Hardly! In fact, they took his life at a time when it seemed that the Church and his family could not have needed him more desperately. Yet, in an eternal sense, he was indeed triumphant because he proved true and faithful until the end of his mortal life, never wavering or equivocating, thus ensuring his inheritance in the kingdom of God.

The Savior promises that all who endure well to the end will experience a fullness of joy forever. The small, painful moments of mortality will be swallowed up in a joyful reunion with a loving Father and Savior. It is often difficult, however, to see past present difficulties and look through the telescope of eternal progression. Just as with our blessings, we can name our "crosses" one by one—pain, persecution in its many manifestations, loss of loved ones, rejection by loved ones, loss of employment, loss of good health—the list is as long and varied as the list of all of God's children.

What we must remember is that our trials are not without purpose. God is neither uncaring nor capricious.

> *The Savior promises that all who endure well to the end will experience a fullness of joy forever.*

He says that His "people must be tried in all things, that they may be prepared to receive the glory that I have for them, even the glory of Zion" (D&C 136:31). Our fidelity to righteous principles and to the Savior and His servants carries with it a magnificent promise: "All that my father hath shall be given unto him" (D&C 84:38). Our faith in our eternal future is the antidote for the pain of the trials we go through in the here and now. A fullness of joy cannot be experienced either here *or* there if we allow the pressures of present difficulties to obscure the heavenly horizon.

❧

"For thou, Lord, wilt bless the righteous; with favor wilt thou compass him as with a shield" (Ps. 5:12).

Counsel with the Lord in all thy doings, and he will direct thee for good; yea, when thou liest down at night lie down unto the Lord, that he may watch over you in your sleep; and when thou risest in the morning let thy heart be full of thanks unto God; and if ye do these things, ye shall be lifted up at the last day.

Alma 37:37

The Prophet Joseph Smith gave this counsel regarding prayer: "Seek to know God in your closets, call upon him in the fields. Follow the directions of the Book of Mormon, and pray over, and for your families, your cattle, your flocks, your herds, your corn, and all things you possess; ask the blessing of God upon all your labors, and everything that you engage in" (*Teachings of the Prophet Joseph Smith*, comp. Joseph Fielding Smith [Salt Lake City: Deseret Book, 1976], 247).

When we counsel with the Lord in *all* our doings, we are having conversations with Him about a variety of things. It is good prayer protocol to begin our prayers with thanks; all that we have reason to rejoice over comes from God, so it is always appropriate and fitting to express gratitude for blessings received.

We might occasionally feel hard-pressed to think of something for which we are grateful when negative circumstances are pressing down on us. A few moments of quiet reflection on our knees will bring to our remembrance what might be at first a trickle of thanks—which, when humbly expressed, will open the floodgates of gratitude. We read of a remarkable example of gratitude as the brother of Jared and his traveling companions sailed toward the promised land, driven by heaven-sent favorable winds. Their gratitude knew no bounds: "And they did sing praises unto the Lord; yea, the brother of Jared did sing praises unto the Lord, and he did thank and praise the Lord all the day long; and when the night came, they did not cease to praise the Lord" (Ether 6:9).

Developing a regular habit of morning and evening prayers keeps us connected with Deity. Our families and friends need to know that our prayers in their behalf are consistent and heartfelt. We need to really mean it when we say to family members and friends, "I'll keep you in my prayers."

To His Saints of latter days, the Savior gives this com-

> *A few moments of quiet reflection on our knees will open the floodgates of gratitude.*

mandment: "Pray *always*, lest you enter into temptation and lose your reward" (D&C 31:12; emphasis added). In each case, He used the word *always* rather than *occasionally* or *whenever you feel like it*.

The Lord is interested in all aspects of our lives and He eagerly awaits our daily calls. The Psalmist reminds us of the order and power of consistent prayer: "Evening, and morning, and at noon, will I pray, and cry aloud: and he shall hear my voice" (Ps. 55:17).

❧

"I sought the Lord, and he heard me, and delivered me from all my fears" (Ps. 34:4).

SEEKING JESUS

And now, I would commend you to seek this Jesus of whom the prophets and apostles have written, that the grace of God the Father, and also the Lord Jesus Christ, and the Holy Ghost, which beareth record of them, may be and abide in you forever.

ETHER 12:41

On several occasions during the Lord's mortal ministry He asked this question in various forms: "Whom seek ye?" (John 18:4). It is a question we might well ask ourselves, keeping Moroni's exhortation in this verse of scripture uppermost in our minds when considering our answer: "We seek this Jesus of whom the prophets and apostles have written." The word *seek* implies an earnest search, and the good news is that He is not hard to find. One of the surest ways to find Him is through searching the scriptures.

When we consider the names of our standard works of scripture, all of them reflect the focus of their content—our Savior Jesus Christ. Three of them testify of His coming and His mortal mission—His work and His glory—and the fourth comprises a compilation of His latter-day doctrines and covenants. He is the key figure, the main feature in all of these works; it is of Him that all of the prophets in all of the dispensations testify. His name is prominent and preeminent throughout the pages of these works. In the Book of Mormon alone, more than one-half of all the verses refer to the Lord, and He is given more than one hundred different names. *He is not hard to find.*

Many things that we seek for in this life are elusive, like a shell game where we are never quite sure about which "shell" to choose. If we make the right choice, the "prize" is ours, but the odds are not necessarily in our favor. We are never completely sure about the outcome of our temporal endeavors because the targets can move and the rules can change.

Contrast this with the countless invitations the Savior extends to us to find Him. "Draw near unto me and I will draw near unto you; seek me diligently and ye shall find me" (D&C 88:63); "Behold, he sendeth an invitation unto all men, for the arms of mercy are extended towards them. . . . Yea, he saith: Come unto me and ye shall partake of the fruit of the tree of life" (Alma 5:33–34). To disciples everywhere, the Sav-

> *The word "seek" implies an earnest search, and the good news is that He is not hard to find.*

ior issues this invitation: "Come, follow me" (Luke 18:22), and His footprints are clear and easy to find throughout the scriptures. He never covers His tracks in order to confuse or deceive or disappoint us. He promises that our search will always be successful; we will always find Him, and the eternal outcome is wondrous. We will be partakers of the Lord's grace and enjoy the companionship of the Holy Ghost—a glorious prize indeed.

"Jesus, our only joy be thou, As thou our prize wilt be;

Jesus, be thou our glory now, And thru eternity" (*Hymns*, no. 141).

⁑

"When thou saidst, Seek ye my face; my heart said unto thee, Thy face, Lord, will I seek" (Ps. 27:8).

WITNESSES OF CHRIST

And this is my doctrine, and it is the doctrine which the Father hath given unto me; and I bear record of the Father, and the Father beareth record of me, and the Holy Ghost beareth record of the Father and me; and I bear record that the Father commandeth all men, everywhere, to repent and believe in me.

3 NE. 11:32

The scriptural law of witnesses is well-known and thoroughly documented: "In the mouth of two or three witnesses shall every word be established" (D&C 6:28). The Father, the Son, and the Holy Ghost stand at all times as witnesses of one another. Every major religious event has been validated and confirmed through this law of witnesses.

Prior to the Savior's birth, numerous prophets testified of His advent. This list of witnesses is long, but we will examine two outstanding examples. Isaiah's prophecies in the Old Testament are well-known and oft-quoted: "For unto us a child is born . . . The mighty God, The everlasting Father, The Prince of Peace" (Isa. 9:6). Samuel the Lamanite prophet left no doubt as to his knowledge of the coming of the Messiah into the world: "Behold, I give unto you a sign; for five years more cometh, and behold, then cometh the Son of God to redeem all those who shall believe on his name" (Hel. 14:2).

On the occasion of this glorious event, there was an abundance of witnesses, including shepherds; heavenly hosts who sang praises at His coming; Wise Men from the East; Simeon and Anna, who saw the infant Jesus in the temple; and Mary and Joseph, for whom this event was so deeply significant. As the Savior began His mortal ministry, He called twelve special witnesses who were privileged to walk and talk with Him. These Twelve sat with Him as He spoke of His impending death, and eleven of them witnessed that awful scene. These same men, along with several women, witnessed the risen and glorified Lord after His Resurrection. So strong was their witness that many of them willingly gave their lives for the cause of their Lord and Savior.

In our own day, Apostles and prophets of God bear solemn and firm

The scriptural law of witnesses is well-known and thoroughly documented.

witness of the divinity of Christ and of His divine Sonship. The scriptures also stand as witnesses of Jesus Christ, and no scripture bears a more valiant and complete witness than the Book of Mormon. First three witnesses and then eight others were called to bear testimony of this ancient record, which stands with its companion, the Holy Bible, as a second witness for Christ.

We too are privileged to be witnesses for Christ. We must decide for ourselves who He is, and then live so our every action stands as our witness of His divinity and of our gratitude and reverence for His saving grace.

❧

"And in the mouth of three witnesses shall these things be established; and . . . all this shall stand as a testimony against the world at the last day" (Ether 5:4).

181

PUT ON THE ARMOR OF RIGHTEOUSNESS

Awake, my sons; put on the armor of righteousness. Shake off the chains with which ye are bound, and come forth out of obscurity, and arise from the dust.

2 NE. 1:23

Lehi highly recommends "the armor of righteousness," and the imagery has a familiar ring, as does the message. The Apostle Paul talks about putting on the whole armor of God (see Eph. 6:11–12), and the Lord provides the details of this armor. Its light and protective spiritual material contrasts dramatically with the heavy metal trappings of the armor worn by knights of old. We are told, "Stand, therefore, having your loins girt about with truth, having on the breastplate of righteousness, and your feet shod with the preparation of the gospel of peace, . . . taking the shield of faith wherewith ye shall be able to quench all the fiery darts of the wicked; And take the helmet of salvation, and the sword of my Spirit" (D&C 27:16–18).

The combined strength of the components of the armor of righteousness is more than sufficient to enable us to shake off Satan's chains—which comprise principalities of darkness and wickedness in all its nefarious forms and diverse places (see Eph. 6:4–12)—to walk uprightly rather than struggle in the dust. Basically the call to put on the armor of righteousness is a call to repentance. Satan would have us believe that there is fame and fortune awaiting us in a future spent with him; however, he advertises no protective armor that guarantees the fulfillment of his empty promises. There is only the ominous clank of his chains that would bind us to a destination of obscurity. The armor of righteousness gives us the strength to shake off his chains, to arise and move upward toward God—toward a celestial destination.

President Spencer W. Kimball urges us as Latter-day Saints to recognize that none of us is immune from the need to repent (see *The Miracle of Forgiveness* [Salt Lake City: Bookcraft, 1969], 31). Repentance is one of the first principles of the gospel of Jesus Christ. The Prophet Joseph Smith taught that "Repentance is a thing that cannot be trifled with every day. Daily transgressions and daily repentance is not that which is pleasing in the sight of God" (*Teachings of the Prophet Joseph Smith*, comp. Joseph Fielding Smith [Salt Lake City: Deseret Book, 1976], 148). It is, indeed, a principle with a promise of the Lord's help and forgiveness. The Lord's armor of righteousness is tailored to every individual's size and needs; it fits each one of us perfectly and comfortably, and fits us for the kingdom of God.

> *The Lord's armor of righteousness is tailored to every individual's size and needs; it fits each one of us perfectly.*

❧

Repentance is a most joyful and universal principle of the gospel, and its application and promise is sure for everyone, regardless of our progress on the pathway to perfection.

"Even As I Am"

Therefore, what manner of men ought ye to be? Verily I say unto you, even as I am.

3 Ne. 27:27

The Savior is the Son of God, and we are but mere mortals, with limitations on our time and talents and capacities. How can we possibly live up to this expectation?

As we ponder this question in our own minds, we come to see that everything the Savior did was an act of service and love and compassion. He reached out with perfect kindness to heal those bowed down by the weight of physical and spiritual infirmities. There was no hesitation on His part; He was never too busy or distracted by His own needs to turn away those who sought His love and attention, whether it was a little child, a hungry multitude, a lonely sinner, or one who suffered the ostracism of a socially repulsive disease.

We are admonished by the Lord to "Remember faith, virtue, knowledge, temperance, patience, brotherly kindness, godliness, charity, humility, diligence" (D&C 4:6). Again, the list seems a bit daunting, but taken one step at a time—one selfless act at a time—it becomes a realistic goal.

We see all about us examples of those who heed this admonition in quiet, selfless acts of service to their fellow men, never begrudging the time spent and never looking for public applause. Take, for example, the home teacher who took time out from a busy schedule of studies and his own family responsibilities to attend the basketball games of a young lady whose own father had abdicated his responsibilities; who included her brother in priesthood activities and outings as if he were one of his own sons; and who never, in all his small acts of kindness, made this fatherless family feel like they were a "project" or a statistic or a burden. They received and welcomed his Christlike overtures with grateful hearts.

Consider the kindness of a ward member who regularly and anonymously supplied a struggling single mother with the finest cuts of meat that provided the basis for many delicious and nutritious meals for her family. Consider too the visiting teacher whose kindness and concern and acts of friendship continued even when her assignment and route changed.

> *We see all about us examples of those who heed this admonition in quiet, selfless acts of service to their fellow men.*

Ponder the generosity of a woman who, despite the fact that she and her husband often struggled to make ends meet in their own family, always had a "little something" on hand to share with a family who might not have much of a Christmas.

What manner of men and women ought we to be? The Savior's example is encouraging rather than discouraging, and His helping hand reaches out to hold our hands when we extend them to others in charity and brotherly kindness.

"By this shall all men know that ye are my disciples, if ye have love one to another" (John 13:35).

Our Savior's Love

But behold, the Lord hath redeemed my soul from hell; I have beheld his glory, and am encircled about eternally in the arms of his love.

2 Ne. 1:15

What can be more pleasing than a hug, especially from a family member or a friend? It is a warm gesture that gives us a feeling of comfort and safety. The Savior is very fond of giving hugs. The scriptures bear witness of this: "Be faithful and diligent in keeping the commandments of God, and I will encircle thee in the arms of my love" (D&C 6:20).

Artists depict the Savior with His arms open and outstretched. There are no pictures of Him with His arms behind His back, or hanging down at His sides, or folded imperviously. He beckons to us and longs to extend the embrace that will bring hope and healing and comfort into our lives. He longs for us to take those steps that move us into His open and inviting embrace.

It is always exciting to receive an invitation to attend some noteworthy event; we feel honored to have been remembered and included. The Savior always includes. We read in Alma 5:33: "Behold, he sendeth an invitation unto all men, for the arms of mercy are extended towards them, and he saith: Repent, and I will receive you." Notice that the invitation is to *all* men and women, not just to a select and intimate few. And what is the special occasion or event to which the Savior extends such a generous invitation? It is the opportunity to share in His glory, to partake of eternal life in His kingdom, to inherit the mansion that He has prepared for our eternal comfort and enjoyment, to feel the warmth of His welcoming embrace.

Invitations usually request a reply, and the RSVP for the Savior's invitation is our willingness to repent. Each repentant act brings an encouraging hug from our Savior as we draw ever closer to His final and eternal embrace. He will never hold us at arm's length, just as we would never hold a child at arm's length, waiting until she gets everything just right. Our Savior reminds us that it is truly possible for us to repent and be forgiven of our sins. We read in Isaiah 1:18, "Come now, and let us reason together, saith the Lord: though your sins be as scarlet, they shall be as white as snow; though they be red like crimson, they shall be as wool." He also promises us

> *He longs for us to take those steps that move us into His open and inviting embrace.*

that our past sins will not be a topic of conversation for Him: "All his transgressions that he hath committed, they shall not be mentioned unto him" (Ezek. 18:22).

We can rest assured that as we feel the Savior's arms around us, He will not be whispering in our ear to remind us of past sins and regrets. His only words will be those He spoke in Matthew 25:21: "Well done, thou good and faithful servant . . . enter thou into the joy of thy Lord" (and His eternal embrace).

"Come unto Jesus, ye heavy laden
Care-worn and fainting, by sin oppressed.
He'll safely guide you unto that haven
Where all who trust him may rest" (Hymns, no. 117).

GLORYING IN OUR LORD

Therefore, let us glory, yea, we will glory in our Lord; yea we will rejoice, for our joy is full; yea, we will praise our God forever. Behold, who can glory too much in the Lord? Yea, who can say too much of his great power, and of his mercy, and of his long-suffering towards the children of men? Behold, I say unto you, I cannot say the smallest part which I feel.

ALMA 26:16

The poet William Wordsworth penned these familiar words:

Our birth is but a sleep and a forgetting;
The Soul that rises with us, our life's Star,
Hath had elsewhere its setting,
And cometh from afar:
Not in entire forgetfulness,
And not in utter nakedness,
But trailing clouds of glory do we come
From God, who is our home:
Heaven lies about us in our infancy! ("Ode on Intimations of Immortality from Recollections of Early Childhood," in Arthur T. Quiller-Couch, ed., *The Oxford Book of English Verse 1250–1900* [Oxford: Clarenden, 1919]).

The phrase *trailing clouds of glory* is most remarkable when we stop to think of our heavenly home. We arrived here from a glorious premortal existence where we enjoyed the company of our Heavenly Father and Mother and our Elder Brother, Jesus Christ. When the veil of mortality was drawn, we no longer remembered the details of that wondrous association, but we definitely arrived at our earthly destination with a spark of divinity, which is called the Light of Christ—our cloud of glory, so to speak. That Light warms and expands our spirits in preparation for the reception of yet more light and knowledge. Our "cloud of glory" then expands to include the gift of the Holy Ghost, which in turn bears witness to us that Jesus Christ is the Son of God our Eternal Father.

Like Ammon, we then come to recognize His great power and mercy. Enlightened by the power of testimony and faith in the Lord Jesus Christ, our joyful boasting

> *We expand in an appreciation for Him that becomes joyful boasting as we enumerate His remarkable and tender mercies.*

is never misplaced or ill-advised, but rather it is aligned with the Lord's admonition: "Wherefore, let no man glory in man, but rather let him glory in God" (D&C 76:61).

We may not have the same profound kinds of missionary experiences as did Ammon and his companions; however, we can joyfully share our testimonies with our spouses, our children, and our friends both in and out of the Church. The Lord approves of our joy, and He eagerly awaits our return to Him, where "our forgetting" will be replaced with full remembrance, and we will bask in the full glory of immortality and eternal life.

"Thy mercy, O Lord, is in the heavens; and thy faithfulness reacheth unto the clouds" (Ps. 36:5).

CLOTHED WITH PURITY

And the righteous shall have a perfect knowledge of their enjoyment, and their righteousness, being clothed with purity, yea, even with the robe of righteousness.

2 NE. 9:14

Personal purity is a process, not an event; it is a lifelong endeavor to draw nearer to God by what we think, say, and, yes, even by what we wear. Purity is prerequisite to donning robes of righteousness, both in the literal and in the figurative sense. It is well for us to bear in mind, however, that any efforts we make in the purification process are totally reliant on the Savior's Atonement, without which we could not hope to be washed clean.

Purity in thought is harder than it sounds. We might congratulate ourselves on never thinking lascivious or immoral thoughts, and that is certainly to be commended. But do we think *unkind* thoughts—things we would never dream of saying out loud to someone, but thoughts that nevertheless privately demean another person's appearance, intellect, or overall worth as a child of God? Do our smiling and pleasant countenances belie an underlying meanness of spirit? The Lord often spoke of cleansing the inner vessel. If we were to be figuratively turned inside out, would we be comfortable with what others would see?

All too frequently, what is in our minds comes out of our mouths. Perhaps it is a tidbit of gossip that casts aspersion on someone else; perhaps an off-color joke or "colorful" language that we reserve for really stressful situations.

Purity in dress is also a reflection of the inner vessel. We can go to either extreme in our attire—too casual or too ornate. Book of Mormon prophets warned against apparel that lifted the wearer up in pride and detracted from the weightier matters of the kingdom. We are also cautioned that apparel that is too casual can cause us to also be too casual in our worship. President David O. McKay counseled us that we should remember that entering a Church building is like entering into the presence of Heavenly Father. Therefore, our thoughts, words, behavior, and clothing should be appropriate for such an encounter (see *Improvement Era*, July 1962, 509).

Modesty and moderation purify our hearts and prepare us for our robes of righteousness. Our

> *Personal purity is a process, not an event; it is a lifelong endeavor to draw nearer to God.*

hearts become pure as we embrace the ordinances of the gospel and manifest our obedience in our thoughts and words and actions—one thought, word, and deed at a time, knowing that our Savior's Atonement has the power to heal, cleanse, and purify us. The words of one of our beloved hymns offer a gentle and hopeful reminder of the Savior's role in our plea for purity:

"More purity give me, More strength to o'er come,
More freedom from earth-stains, More longing for home.
More fit for the kingdom, More used would I be,
More blessed and holy—More, Savior, like thee" (*Hymns*, no. 131).

"*The words of the pure are pleasant words*" (Prov. 15:26).

CHILDREN OF CHRIST

And moreover, I say unto you, that there shall be no other name given nor any other way nor means whereby salvation can come unto the children of men, only in and through the name of Christ, the Lord Omnipotent.

MOSIAH 3:17

As members of The Church of Jesus Christ of Latter-day Saints, we look forward to those two special times of the year when general conference is convened. During those times, all may hear the words of prophets, seers, and revelators and other General Authorities as they bear witness of Jesus Christ—the Way, the Truth, and the Life. We tune our hearts and minds so that we can enjoy a heart-to-heart encounter. Then, once the conference is over, we eagerly await the Church publications, when we can again savor these inspirational addresses through the printed word.

In the pages of the Book of Mormon we read of a momentous general conference that was convened by that great prophet-king, Benjamin, more than a hundred years before the birth of Christ. The people gathered in their families and pitched their tents with their doors facing the temple so that they could see and hear the proceedings of the conference. The multitude was so great that even though King Benjamin erected a tower from which to deliver his sermon, he also had the printed word distributed among the people so that they could follow along during his sermon and also savor his words after they returned to their homes. The content and theme of this conference was sacred, much of it revealed to King Benjamin by an angel of the Lord, who came to declare to him "the glad tidings of great joy" (Mosiah 3:3), words that an angel of the Lord declared to shepherds on a hillside in Bethlehem many years later. The message was the same in each case—it was the heavenly testimony and declaration of the birth of the Son of God and His mission of mercy and Atonement in behalf of all His children, regardless of when and where they had lived or would ever live.

So sacred was this message of hope, so glad were these tidings, so firmly did all the people believe their prophet's testimony and message of salvation that comes only in and through the name of Jesus Christ that they were willing to take upon themselves Christ's name and become His faithful followers. They became the children of Christ and were anxious to have their names so recorded on the records of the Church.

> *It is our sacred privilege to have the Savior's name written in our hearts as we faithfully remember Him.*

That conference was a glorious experience for those faithful members. Like Book of Mormon Saints of old, it is our sacred privilege to have the Savior's name written in our hearts, and to have our names recorded in His book of life as we faithfully remember Him and keep His commandments.

✢

"And now, behold, my beloved brethren, this is the way; and there is none other way nor name given under heaven whereby man can be saved in the kingdom of God" (2 Ne. 31:21).

Song of Redeeming Love 98

And now behold, I say unto you, my brethren, if ye have experienced a change of heart, and if ye have felt to sing the song of redeeming love, I would ask, can ye feel so now?

Alma 5:26

The message of the gospel is a joyful and hopeful message; it fills us with the love of God and invites reverence for our Redeemer. It is, as the Apostle Paul so boldly declares, "the power of God unto salvation to every one that believeth" (Rom. 1:16). It has the power to change lives and hearts. In fact, the whole purpose of the gospel is to change lives; if we had no need for change, there would be no need for a Redeemer.

We experience that change only through repentance. We are reminded of Paul's words: "All have sinned, and come short of the glory of God" (Rom. 3:23). How very great, then, is our need for a Redeemer, as attested to by Nephi: "Wherefore, all mankind were in a lost and in a fallen state, and ever would be save they should rely on this Redeemer" (1 Ne. 10:6).

Reliance on our Redeemer requires a changed heart. Our priorities become more Christ-centered, and our thoughts and actions are altered accordingly. It is an ongoing process that requires a prayerful commitment to the Lord and a prayerful recommitment to our covenants. It is this process that teaches us "the song of redeeming love."

Alma was very familiar with the lyrics and music of the song of redeeming love, having changed from being one of the vilest of sinners to being one of God's most faithful servants. When he remembered the words of his father regarding Jesus Christ, who would come to atone for the sins of the world, he cried out in his heart, pleading for mercy and forgiveness. Only then was he released from "the pains of a damned soul," and his "soul was filled with joy as exceeding as was [his] pain." He thought he saw "God sitting upon his throne," and he longed to be with the "numberless concourses of angels, in the attitude of singing and praising their God" (Alma 36:16–20).

We can easily relate to the contrasting feelings we have when we fall short and when we measure up. No one feels like singing when things are not going well; the best we can muster at those times is a melancholy monotone. However, when we put our lives in order, the melody is spontaneous,

> *Alma was very familiar with the lyrics of the song of redeeming love, having become one of God's most faithful servants.*

pure, and joyful, regardless of our level of musical expertise. It is spontaneous because we are filled with the love of God, we are filled with a "knowledge of that which is just and true" (Mosiah 4:12); it is pure because we are cleansed by the Savior's Atonement; it is joyful "because of the resurrection of the dead, according to the will and power and deliverance of Jesus Christ from the bands of death" (Alma 4:14). We are not ashamed to let anyone—especially the Savior—listen to our song.

"Savior, Redeemer of my soul, Whose mighty hand hath made me whole, Whose wondrous pow'r hath raised me up And filled with sweet my bitter cup! What tongue my gratitude can tell, O gracious God of Israel" (Hymns, no. 112).

ASKING AND BELIEVING

And whatsoever ye shall ask the Father in my name, which is right, believing that ye shall receive, behold it shall be given unto you.

3 Ne. 18:20

The Savior's ministry among the Nephites was a time of exquisite joy for the people who had been spared from the terrible destruction that had come upon the land at the time of the Savior's Crucifixion. They heard the Father's voice bearing witness of His Son, in whom He was well pleased; they were privileged to feel the wounds in the hands and feet of the resurrected Lord; they learned about baptism and the sacrament; they listened with quiet reverence to the Sermon on the Mount; they experienced firsthand the Savior's healing hand; they watched as angels encircled their little ones after they had been individually blessed by the Savior; and they were given personal and generous blessings almost too numerous to mention, some of which were too sacred to record.

It was also a time of exquisite joy for the Savior. He tenderly expressed His feelings to the multitude: "Blessed are ye because of your faith. And now behold, my joy is full" (3 Ne. 17:20).

Among the blessings that the Savior bestowed upon the Nephites was His promise that nothing would be withheld from them if they asked in faith for that which was right.

Was this a special boon granted to only a few chosen members of the Lord's flock? Moroni makes it clear that this is not the case: "Behold, I say unto you that whoso believeth in Christ, doubting nothing, whatsoever he shall ask the Father in the name of Christ it shall be granted him; *and this promise is unto all, even unto the ends of the earth*" (Morm. 9:21; emphasis added).

> *Ask in faith, and ask for that which is right. The Lord will then withhold nothing from us.*

The Lord is fair in the way He treats all of His children, and the conditions of fulfillment of this promise are the same for all of us: ask in faith, and ask for that which is right. The Lord will then withhold nothing from us.

The Nephites believed the Savior's promise; the brother of Jared believed the Savior's promise; and we believe His promise because we know that He lives and loves us. He desires to give us the righteous desires of our hearts, that our joy might also be full.

✤

"Then shalt thou call, and the Lord shall answer; thou shalt cry, and he shall say, Here I am" (Isa. 58:9).

Testimony of the Book of Mormon

Behold, I would exhort you that when you shall read these things, if it be wisdom in God that ye should read them, that ye would remember how merciful the Lord hath been unto the children of men, from the creation of Adam even down until the time that ye shall receive these things, and ponder it in your hearts. And when ye shall receive these things, I would exhort you that ye would ask God, the Eternal Father, in the name of Christ, if these things are not true; and if ye shall ask with a sincere heart, with real intent, having faith in Christ, he will manifest the truth of it unto you, by the power of the Holy Ghost. And by the power of the Holy Ghost ye may know the truth of all things.

MORONI 10:3–5

The Prophet Joseph Smith, who translated the Book of Mormon by the gift and power of God, declared that it "was the most correct of any book on earth, and the keystone of our religion, and a man would get nearer to God by abiding by its precepts, than by any other book" (*Teachings of the Prophet Joseph Smith*, comp. Joseph Fielding Smith [Salt Lake City: Deseret Book, 1976], 194). It is Another Testament of Jesus Christ, and the Lord Himself bears testimony of its truthfulness: "As your Lord and your God liveth it is true" (D&C 17:6). It is humbling to have His sacred witness and to be reminded by Moroni that we are privileged to have this record because of the Lord's tender mercy.

The Book of Mormon was written for our time; it is the

word of God, compiled and faithfully recorded by ancient prophets and record-keepers. It is a complementary companion to the Holy Bible, and it contains the fulness of the gospel of Jesus Christ.

Throughout the pages of the Book of Mormon, prophets bear testimony of the truthfulness of this sacred record. Nephi declares that the "things which [he has] written are true" (1 Ne. 14:30). Alma testifies of "the records which are true" (Alma 3:12). King Benjamin tells his sons of the records that "they are true; and we can know of a surety because we have them before our eyes" (Mosiah 1:6). Moroni, the last of the Nephite record-keepers, bears solemn witness that the contents of the Book of Mormon are true, and he gives us the key by which we too can gain a testimony of its truthfulness.

> *Moroni gives us the key by which we can gain a testimony of the truthfulness of the Book of Mormon.*

Moroni invites us to put the Book of Mormon to the test by asking God. In essence, Moroni is telling us that we don't have to take his or anyone else's word for it; we can go directly to the Author of all truth. But he cautions us that our petitions must be sincere, based on faith in Christ, and the intent of our heart must be rooted in a deep desire for truth. Only then will the Holy Ghost bear witness to us that "these things are true."

❧

"But he that believeth these things which I have spoken, him will I visit with the manifestations of my Spirit, and he shall know and bear record. For because of my Spirit he shall know that these things are true; for it persuadeth men to do good" (Ether 4:11).

About the Author

Shauna Kaye Humphreys was born in Cardston, Alberta, Canada. She is a graduate of Brigham Young University with a bachelor of science degree and a master of arts degree in English. A professional editor, she has taught in the public schools and has also taught writing and composition courses at Brigham Young University and Utah Valley University. Shauna has served as a stake Primary president, as a counselor in Relief Society, and as a teacher in various Church auxiliaries. She has also taught early-morning seminary for many years, and currently enjoys team-teaching gospel doctrine class with her dear husband, Rick. They live in Birch Bay, Washington, and share the joys of their combined family of nine children and thirteen grandchildren.